CW00554389

'*Positively Purple* is a tale abou
of people with disabilities. Any
robustness of their disability stra
politics of disability. Kate's pers
honesty, is a compelling read and full of practical lessons.'
DUNCAN TAIT, CHIEF EXECUTIVE, INCHCAPE PLC

'*Positively Purple* should be required reading for every FTSE
250 CEO. Business leaders need to understand and value
"human capital". Kate is an expert in helping us recognise
the value of *every* human – including those with disabilities.'
IAN STUART, CHIEF EXECUTIVE OFFICER, HSBC UK BANK PLC

'Global multinationals like GSK increasingly choose to
learn directly from their employees with disabilities. Building
disability confidence from the inside out by investing in a
disability employee resource group will make the journey so
much easier. Kate's personal story shows us how to supercharge the disability inclusion revolution and create a better,
more accessible, working world.' ANDY GARRETT, WORKPLACE
ADJUSTMENTS SERVICE PROGRAMME DIRECTOR AND GLOBAL
CO-LEAD DISABILITY CONFIDENCE NETWORK – EMPLOYEE
RESOURCE GROUP, GSK

'It's hard for me to talk about Kate and her work without
sounding like I am always using hyperbole. I find Kate's presence throughout *Positively Purple* inspiring. Her words
embolden the reader to participate as proactive protagonists in the fight for equity. The path she outlines uses
lessons from other equality and identity dimensions but
adds a particular magic, unique to Kate herself. This book
is essential reading for anyone who would call themselves
an ally of equity at work. My team and I are all avid fans of

Kate and grateful for all her lessons and practical actions.' JOHN AMAECHI OBE, FOUNDER, APS INTELLIGENCE

'Kate has managed to do what no one before her has ever done. *Positively Purple* is the manuscript for living life and creating epic change for people with disabilities. Kate's special brand of combined grace and spicy wit helps us quite literally feel better for life. She has taught us how to feel good and change the world simultaneously as shown by empirical data. Prepare to have a hard time putting the book down.' BELINDA MAY, PARTNER AND CO-CHAIR OF US DISABILITIES/ACCESSIBILITY EMPLOYEE RESOURCE GROUP

'*Positively Purple* is an incredibly powerful and positive view into Kate's world and the invaluable work she continues to do to raise awareness of the challenges millions face daily. Kate delves into the world of work, which for many is a minefield, and opens the door by providing tangible suggestions for people with disabilities and those who are looking to hire the best talent!' STEVE INGHAM, CHIEF EXECUTIVE, PAGEGROUP

'An unrelentingly positive read! Brilliantly weaves her story with the must-read practical advice for employers. Show how employers can lead as allies to create a powerful movement for change, in delivering an inclusive workplace and society.' MARK HODGKINSON, CHIEF EXECUTIVE, SCOPE

'There is nothing inevitable about progress – it takes relentless campaigning and great campaigners. Kate is one of those people. Her insights into how to create a space without fear of getting it wrong and the importance of positive campaigning should be read by every social change campaigner.' TIERNAN BRADY, GLOBAL DIRECTOR OF INCLUSION,CLIFFORD CHANCE LLP

Positively Purple

*Build an inclusive world where people
with disabilities can flourish*

Kate Nash

Publisher's note
Every possible effort has been made to ensure that the information contained in this book is accurate at the time of going to press, and the publishers and author cannot accept responsibility for any errors or omissions, however caused. No responsibility for loss or damage occasioned to any person acting, or refraining from action, as a result of the material in this publication can be accepted by the editor, the publisher or the author.

First published in Great Britain and the United States in 2023 by Kogan Page Limited

Apart from any fair dealing for the purposes of research or private study, or criticism or review, as permitted under the Copyright, Designs and Patents Act 1988, this publication may only be reproduced, stored or transmitted, in any form or by any means, with the prior permission in writing of the publishers, or in the case of reprographic reproduction in accordance with the terms and licences issued by the CLA. Enquiries concerning reproduction outside these terms should be sent to the publishers at the undermentioned addresses:

2nd Floor, 45 Gee Street
London
EC1V 3RS
United Kingdom
www.koganpage.com

8 W 38th Street, Suite 902
New York, NY 10018
USA

4737/23 Ansari Road
Daryaganj
New Delhi 110002
India

Kogan Page books are printed on paper from sustainable forests.

© Purple Space Ltd, 2023

ISBNs
Hardback   978 1 3986 0849 8
Paperback   978 1 3986 0847 4
Ebook   978 1 3986 0848 1

British Library Cataloguing-in-Publication Data
A CIP record for this book is available from the British Library.

Library of Congress Cataloging-in-Publication Data
Names: Nash, Kate (Disabilities trainer & consultant), author
Title: Positively purple : build an inclusive world where people with disabilities can flourish / Kate Nash.
Description: London, United Kingdom ; New York, NY : Kogan Page, 2022. | Includes bibliographical references and index.
Identifiers: LCCN 2022031794 (print) | LCCN 2022031795 (ebook) | ISBN 9781398608474 (paperback) | ISBN 9781398608498 (hardback) | ISBN 9781398608481 (ebook)
Subjects: LCSH: People with disabilities–Employment. | Diversity in the workplace. | Discrimination against people with disabilities.
Classification: LCC HD7255 .N29 2022 (print) | LCC HD7255 (ebook) | DDC 362.4/0484–dc23/eng/20220713
LC record available at https://lccn.loc.gov/2022031794
LC ebook record available at https://lccn.loc.gov/2022031795

Typeset by Hong Kong FIVE Workshop
Print production managed by Jellyfish
Printed and bound by CPI Group (UK) Ltd, Croydon, CR0 4YY

To Mum and Dad, for their patience and care and unswerving support. They lived largely for their kids. The older I get the more I realize, apparently, that's not a gift that everyone receives.

To Susan Scott-Parker OBE who lit the fire. Call the fire brigade. This fire can't be extinguished, and we all blame you.

To Kay Allen OBE, my kick-ass, weird and wonderful friend and personal coach who eyeballs and advises ministers and company chief executives at the same time as mucking out the pig shed. Neither pigs nor FTSE 100 companies are harmed in the process.

To Mark Jones and the band of remarkable boys and girls that make up our family shape: Gareth, Marc, Owen, Amy, Elsie and Heidi. You are so real and lovely that even the roots of my hair tingle.

CONTENTS

Preface

When movements take off

Summer 2017. PurpleSpace, the world's only leadership development hub for disability employee resource group (ERG)/network leaders, was growing in front of my very eyes. It was less than two years old. Businesses were queuing up to join the community. They wanted to invest in the process of building disability confidence from the inside out via the creation of ERGs/networks. The early adopters included Barclays, GSK, Fujitsu, PwC and Lloyds Banking Group, and many more were joining. We could not keep up with demand.

Sitting in my central London home-office, I reflected on my journey to date. In 1978, as a 15-year-old teen, newly diagnosed with juvenile rheumatoid arthritis, my life fell apart. I could not walk, dress myself or feed myself because I was in constant pain. To move would be to be in pain. I experienced a dramatic onset of a disease I thought only 'older people' got. I was in and out of hospital, my family was disrupted, my future unclear. Three years later, when trying to get into university and unsure about my future job prospects, my mother said to me, 'It would be nice, one day, if you could get a *little* job.' It was said with love, though the subtext was for me not to get too ambitious, that I may not get or sustain a job (more about my brilliant mum later). The river of tears went inwards. The sadness of others was too great to accommodate any room for mine.

Decades later as I scrolled through my Twitter feed during the LGBT+ Pride Month of June 2017 it struck me how most successful people movements are led by the people most impacted by injustice. At 54, I had managed to work through a succession of ever-larger jobs, and along the way seen attitudes across the world to disabled employees change over four decades. Some of those changes were down to my own, personal efforts. I'd gone a long way by never taking no for an answer.

PurpleSpace, a small social business with a very big mission, had been the natural progression of these efforts. Our name had been inspired by using colour to create a powerful brand, just as the rainbow flag is now synonymous with the Pride movement and the so-called 'grey pound' signifies the buying strength of the older community. We had been the first to inspire disability ERGs to do that. Others were starting to follow.

I knew that using colour – and ensuring disability ERGs felt unified in their leadership during 3 December, the annual UN International Day of Persons with Disabilities – was going to be vital in building a bigger global community around a human experience which most individuals who have that experience would prefer not to have. That isn't always a popular thing to say since we have all grown up with the social model of disability as our symbolic North Star – our Polaris has served as a beacon of inspiration and hope for a more equitable world for people with disabilities.

I wondered about the millions of people who had been permanently drowned by their tears: those less lucky in meeting fellow travellers who see disability as a political experience, not a medical one and who shout 'keep going' in our ears when life is super-tough. The millions who must first 'prove' the things they cannot do in order to secure income support or social care support and then 'prove' their brilliance to get the first job. These things conspire to build a realistic narrative about the complexity of our lives.

I reflected too on the role of the business community in building an accessible working world. Sustained change does not come from skilful diversity and inclusion managers alone: important (though rare) as they are. Nor does it come from hero CEOs who might be persuaded to sign a charter and 'play' with disability as flavour of the month. Nor from charities. Nor do work and independence come from the skills of doctors or social workers or the quality of legislation. And the speed of change certainly does not come from 'better monitoring' or more sophisticated ways to try and count how many disabled people you employ: what is often called the 'disclosure' or 'declaration' of disability (a lot more about this later!) Nor does systemic change come from conducting a benchmarking standard or indexing corporate progress each year.

In that Pride month, watching my Twitter feed come alive with the rainbow flag, I felt the enduring truth that progress in human rights only ever comes when those adversely impacted by an experience create global networks, share their lived experiences and choose to lean in and act to help those that come behind us. When they say, 'no more'. The next raft of change was going to be driven by people with disabilities already in work. Economics talks. Money talks. People with disabilities in work must talk.

My working life was far from over, but I always have my eye on the end game. PurpleSpace was growing and our conscious choice to use colour to signify community was paying off. We'd been building the leadership capability and sense of community among the many disability ERGs we'd helped create and who subsequently improved business performance. But what would it take to supercharge a movement for change – one based on a more positive narrative about our lives? One that celebrated our contribution to economies around the globe. One that counteracted the 'Mis-Dis-information' about how challenging our lives always are (more later).

I was still scrolling through Twitter and reading the brilliant, upbeat, celebratory tweets about how the LGBT+ community were leading systemic change. Dozens of business buildings were proudly flying the rainbow flag. One tweet showed a picture of the Merseyside Police HQ in Liverpool, where the impressive stone columns were each lit up in a different colour of the rainbow. Another tweet exchange took place between a senior figure at Stonewall and the openly gay ERG leader of a major global bank in the United States. It was an inspiring and largely positive narrative which was hard to ignore.

I knew then what I needed to do: disability ERGs and people with disabilities in work needed to feel good about the unique role they play in driving systems change in the very organizations that employ us as part of the United

Nations International Day of Persons with Disabilities. If PurpleSpace had made the colour purple 'famous' around the world in relation to the employment experience of disabled people, then we needed a 'hook' or a 'moment' to unify us and to celebrate our economic contribution.

I picked up my iPhone but what to say in a small number of words? I tapped out a brief tweet.

'What about we start to light up purple on 3 December #IDPWD,' I tweeted, alongside a bright picture of the Merseyside police building bathed in rainbow colours, to drive the message home.[1]

In my wildest dreams, I could never have anticipated the response. This book is about the story of my life as the build-up to #PurpleLightUp, why it was necessary and what I have learnt about how to build a world where people with disabilities can flourish. Through my personal story I offer practical advice to employers and employees alike – though everything I offer is designed to help anyone who may read this book. This may include parents, medics, teachers, parliamentarians, lawyers and the millions of allies around the globe.

I hope my words offer positive and purposeful ideas that we can all deploy to build a better, more accessible world for people with disabilities.

A FEW THANKS

All books start with purpose and this one is no exception. It would not have been written without the influence of many positive and purposeful people who have had a big impact on my life.

The fellow travellers who did much of the heavy lifting to stimulate disability and/or employer movements around the globe and whose efforts helped secure employment legislation as well as those that helped keep up the good fight: the writers, the 'system thinkers', the activists, the uncompromising leaders, the quiet game changers, the loud rule breakers: Baroness Jane Campbell, Liz Carr, Suzanne Colbert AM GAICD, Dr Stephen Duckworth OBE, Phil Friend OBE, Professor David Grayson CBE, Judy Heumann, Simon Minty, Elspeth Morrison, Peter de Oude, Susan Scott-Parker OBE, Ann Stead OBE, Stefan Tromel, Graeme Whippy MBE.

The PurpleSpace staff and consultants who brought and bring the best of themselves to the engine room: Vanessa Hardy, Jo Hussey, Sally Ward, Sarah Simcoe, Lauren Pemberton Nelson, Ed Mylles, Angie Elrick, Brendan Roach, Marilyn Yeboah, Kerry Francis, Angelina McPherson.

The creators, strategic supporters, friends and investors of PurpleSpace: Rob Wemyss, David Hallett, Iain Wilkie, David Shields, David Caldwell, Andy Garrett, Andy Kneen OBE, John Turner, Paul Willgoss MBE, Fleur Bothwick OBE, Gavin Bounds, Mark Hodgkinson, Donna Miller,

Jeff King, Samantha Saunders, Antony Marke, Pank Kora, Tom Frantz, Liz Douglas, Juliet Silvester, Alia Cooper, Tulsi Patel, Darren Rowen, Jamie Mills, Ally, Jeff Dodds, Julian John, Debra Ruh, Neil Milliken, Antonio Vieira Santos, Caroline Casey, Paul Deemer, Dr Hamied Haroon, Janet Hill CBE, John Amaechi OBE, Diane Lightfoot, Sophie Morgan, Sonia Bate, Toby Mildon, Vanessa Vallely OBE, Martyn Sibley, Orla Pearson, Yvonne Smyth, Nasser Siabi OBE.

The HSBC UK 'cavalry' who underpin and lead in equal measure: Sally Williams, Ian Stuart, Sally Owen, Graeme Moffat, Kirstie Wilson, Louise Somerville, Alex Taylor.

For bringing the book into the world, I thank Teena Lyons who made me think very hard, squeezed the story out of me and made me dig deep. For teaching me about the world of publishing I thank Jeff Scott who also helped me to believe that the book was worthy and different and a necessary addition in the world. For saying yes, and for leadership, my sincere thanks to Chris Cudmore and his colleagues at Kogan Page, most especially Susi Lowndes and Jaini Haria. When he got excited, I got excited and excitement motivates you to keep writing, shaping and creating.

And finally, a thank you to the thousands of past, current and future disability employee resource group/network leaders around the world. It is this phenomenal community of internal agitators that will change the working world.

MIND YOUR LANGUAGE

This book is not about the legal definitions of disability, language preferences or what different pieces of legislation require employers to do when it comes to people with disabilities.It is a book about how disabled people get into the workplace, how they stay and progress at work, and what actions employers can take that will bring significant benefits to their business.

The practical advice is woven through the story of my life and career.

Throughout the book I will, without apology, use the terms 'people with disabilities' and 'disabled people'. And in doing so I am referring to many millions of people with disability around the globe. One billion people, or 15 per cent of the world's population, experience some form of disability, and disability prevalence is higher for developing countries. One-fifth of the estimated global total, or between 110 and 190 million people, experience significant disabilities.[1]

Some people will not use the language of disability as part of their identity and will never do so. This will often include people who have been deaf or hard of hearing from birth. It may include people who have experienced a dramatic accident through sporting endeavour, or war, or simply by walking across the road at the wrong time and being hit by a driver not paying enough attention. It will include people who experience a long-term chronic disease such as arthritis. It may include people who have had an unexpected medical diagnosis such as diabetes or multiple sclerosis and with speedy treatment and good medical care may navigate a tough few years before moving into more manageable days. Or not. It may include people who have an inherited genetic condition. It may include people who experience a mental ill-health condition for six months, three years or a lifetime. It may include people with life-limiting conditions, such as cancer or HIV or muscular dystrophy. It may include people who experience facial disfigurement. Or it might include people who consider themselves as neurodivergent: they may have Autistic Spectrum Disorder or one of the many subtypes, such as Asperger's. They may have ADHD or dyslexia, dyscalculia or dyspraxia. The list goes on.

I chose deliberately in this book not to 'educate' readers about language preferences or who is covered by legislation. Some individuals and employers will prefer to use the 'people first' recommendations of the United Nations.[2] Others will prefer to use the 'politics first' preferences of many disabled people. I have my own personal preference when it comes to language though I consciously chose not to spend my limited time on earth by educating others on these issues.

However, if you are tongue-tied and simply don't know what to say or how to start a conversation or are scared about making a mistake, do not worry. You are not alone. And it is OK to make mistakes. If you want to be a better ally, I promise to offer ideas and insights whether you understand the politics of language or not. So, keep reading.

Introduction

All people with a disability have a back story. It is often one that will stay with us until the day we die. It is the foundation upon which we build our reserves of confidence, and this foundation needs to be firm because, whatever happens, people often look at us and perceive us as 'different'. This can be tricky enough to navigate in our personal lives, but in the workplace, where we may encounter hundreds, even thousands of colleagues, contacts, suppliers and customers, breaking down inaccurate assumptions can be a minefield.

I have spent 35 years campaigning for workplace inclusion for disabled people and to build a better and more accessible working world. My goal has always been to invite folk to consider 'disability' in a variety of ways and certainly to see it as a more positive human experience than the most immediate reactions of others may suggest. This, in my mind, is a 'system' challenge as much as an individual reflex action. Along the way I have met and worked alongside some truly remarkable individuals. Some will refer to themselves as 'campaigners' or 'freedom fighters' that have been fully prepared to make a nuisance of themselves in political corridors and helped bring about legislative reform. Others operate more as 'systems thinkers' and 'social psychologists' that create new landscapes by which we can tackle old problems by coming at them from new directions. Others are 'process engineers' tackling the end-to-end workplace adjustment/accommodation process in their organizations. They come from organizations that are genuinely putting boots on the ground to improve systems that make it easier for their people to secure a workplace adjustment/accommodation.

All tactics, methods and crucial moments have played a vital part. Though the fact that there have been significant improvements over three decades or more is not solely down to these incredible people. A huge amount of credit must go to 'ordinary' individuals with disabilities who have stood up and said: 'No more, not in my name.' It is these individuals that I have worked most closely with in recent years, because I have seen first-hand how powerful creating a meaningful dialogue between employer and employee can be. When organizations understand the true lived experiences of their own people, they can work together to change policy, practice and procedure. That is when the magic happens and when people feel more able to bring their authentic selves to work. And when they feel able to do that, the change process accelerates.

Misinformation and disinformation

Anyone who truly wants to be an ally to people with disabilities already in work or looking for work will have to learn how to ignore some of the unhelpful information that is churned out about our lives. 'Misinformation' is a term that refers to false information that is shared without an intent to mislead. 'Disinformation' refers to false information that is shared with an intent to deceive and mislead. I have invented a new word: 'Mis-Dis-information'. This is neither false information shared without intent, nor false information shared with intent. For me, Mis-Dis-information is the constant barrage of disability information that is churned out about how tough our lives are AT ALL TIMES. Go into any Twitter feed and tap in 'disability'. Get prepared to feel gloomy within seconds.

In my view, this type of method of driving change is not helpful any more and is one of the most significant barriers to future change. And while there may be some foundations upon which the 'facts' are offered, such Mis-Dis-information does nothing to offer practical advice to genuine allies who want to build a more accessible working world. Knowing how awful something is rarely leads to systemic change.

News stories that just share more statistics about how few employers employ people with disabilities do little to drive change. News stories and research reports that call out how few senior positions are occupied by people with disabilities do little to drive change. News stories about how hard it is to secure timely workplace adjustments/accommodations do little to drive change.

Don't get me wrong. My view is not that such challenges do not exist and that some research and statistics can help some get a wiggle on. In fact, I will refer to the more helpful studies and ideas that might turn your head. But seriously, is this all there is?

Thirty minutes of scrolling a news feed after a new piece of 'information' is launched leaves you impotent, depressed and largely apathetic. Calling out constant Mis-Dis-information about a particular group of people does little to paint new pictures about what can be done to improve their lives. Every person who reposts a negative story about the experience of disability continues to perpetuate myths and untruths about the full texture of our lives. I am not suggesting we ignore the challenges that remain. But to keep us in the negative storyline will forever *keep* us in the negative storyline. And it does not build a collective understanding of truth. It does nothing but encourage apathetic non-allies to keep doing nothing. Not to mention the fact that it reduces hope and direction to those who experience disability for the first time and who are trying to make sense of a new future.

In his book *Factfulness*, Hans Rosling, with co-authors Ola Rosling and Anna Rosling Ronnlund, reminds us how human beings:[1]

> have a strong and dramatic instinct towards binary thinking, a basic urge to divide things up into two distinct groups, with nothing but an empty gap in between. We love to

dichotomize. Good versus bad. Heroes versus villains. My country versus the rest. Dividing the world into two distinct sides is simple and intuitive, and also dramatic because it implies conflict, and we do it without thinking, all the time.

They go on to share how journalists know this too:

They set up their narratives as conflicts between two opposing people, views or groups. They prefer stories of extreme poverty and billionaires to stories about the vast majority of people slowly dragging themselves towards better lives.

Their first chapter calls out the Mega Misconception that the world is divided in two – that it is the first of our 10 dramatic instincts, the gap instinct: the irresistible temptation we have to divide all kinds of things into two distinct and often conflicting groups.

Factfulness is both a sobering and uplifting read, and especially important for anyone who truly thinks they are changing the world for people with disabilities via a social media repost of yet another deficit-shouting piece of research.

Telling positive stories

Over time I have come to understand the importance of positive storytelling in the workplace. Everybody knows somebody with a disability. Perhaps someone in the family has a health condition, or a close friend or colleague. When people like me tell our individual stories it opens a dialogue between us, which is the first important step in any change process. Chances are, when we vocalize our stories, there will be something in there that most people can relate to. They will know individuals who found a way to keep their job, or get a promotion, or went on to get their next job. They will know individuals who were born with a disability and found it hard to navigate their education and then got a lucky break, simply by first volunteering, then making themselves indispensable. Others with indirect experience may have lobbied their employer to set up a work experience programme and led it as a volunteer alongside the day job. Then years later their own son with cerebral palsy gets his first break as a disabled graduate in the same company. Sharing our lived experiences creates strong, healthy life-affirming relationships. Most importantly, this is how change begins.

When we tell our stories we help our employers become more informed. It helps businesses to create an environment where employees with disability can bring their authentic selves to work and use their talents to the full. It stops the situation where employers simply do their best to keep to the letter of the law or take the 'safe' option of sticking rigidly to mandated 'reasonable adjustment/ accommodation policies'. In most cases, it is not that organizations want to discriminate; quite the opposite in fact. It is just that there is an ever-present fear of asking the wrong question, or inadvertently causing offence. If we all take the initiative and start the conversation, we can embark on a journey of improvement together. We can ditch outdated language such as 'disclose' and 'declare' and move towards the far more inviting process of 'sharing'. I have seen many, many businesses do just this and the result is astounding, benefiting both employees and employers.

Not everyone sees themselves as a campaigner wanting to do their bit in transforming a bit of the world. I know that. However, having the courage to tell a story can be transformational on an individual basis too. I have never forgotten the stark change that I went through when I was diagnosed with Stills disease as a teenager. Overnight, people treated me completely differently to the way they had before. The difference was so jarring that the impact of it has never left me. My experience is by no means unique. Out of all the people with disabilities in the UK workplace, 83 per cent have acquired their condition at some point during their working life.[2] That often means a change of identity. This new identity is not one we actively invite into our lives and certainly not one that we want. We all go through a very different transition period from the before to the after, but what we have in common is that what happens 'after' is driven by want and need. With a newly acquired disability we may need to learn new ways of moving around or managing pain and discomfort. Alternatively, we may even need to find new ways of communicating or getting to grips with other entirely new skills. At the same time, while all this is going on, we need to manage a swathe of other people's disappointment or sadness at our new circumstance. It is very easy to push our feelings about this down deep inside, because it is often just too much. Finding a way to articulate that story is the first step in making sense of this new identity.

In my early days I was not a natural storyteller. I am not the type to breeze into a room and use my story to provoke people into action. I chose deliberately not to deploy 'passion without a plan' – I do not prod and poke with a wobble in my voice. While some may choose to do that and the immediate aftermath can be highly effective, that approach never sat very well with me and it certainly is not a sustainable strategy. I suspect there is a link with one of my earliest jobs where I spoke with numerous youngsters across Europe who all, like me, had arthritis. These wonderful, energetic, committed young adults all had stories to tell. What made my own story any more important? Like many people with disability, I also found it difficult to articulate my experiences, good and bad. It can take a huge amount of courage. That is especially so if it means telling it to someone who means the world to you. I will add that, over time, with the telling and the retelling, it becomes easier. Then, you learn how to say it better and how to deal with the reactions you get. You will realize that saying things to people at the right time, in the right way, starts a constructive conversation and nips any negativity in the bud. Plus, when we are out, loud and proud, it makes it easier for those that come behind us.

In creating PurpleSpace and the #PurpleLightUp movement, celebrating the contribution that employees with disability make all over the world, I have grown used to telling my story. Even so, I am still frequently asked to explain how the purple movement began and why I believe it has super-charged the inclusion revolution – and much more importantly, what can we learn from it in order to improve business performance still further. This is, at least in part, what inspired me to write this book – as well as offering some simple advice to our allies.

There are many parallels in my story that may help others in a similar situation, people who navigate their careers while juggling a personal challenge. The themes I share are the same as thousands of employees with disability I have spoken with over the years. It is my hope that by documenting what I have learnt, this book may provide insights to anyone who is looking for work, or already in paid employment but perhaps struggling, or who simply wants to live a more fulfilled and productive life. Plus, of course, I want as many organizations as possible to hear this story. If my life experience, together with the hints, tips and words of advice I have soaked up over the years from a huge number of amazing people, make things better for those that follow behind me, I will have done my job.

As the title of this book suggests, this is a celebration of talent and what has already been achieved by millions of disabled people in work. I am, as people have often commented, relentlessly positive. I am neither proud nor sorry to be so. That's the way I am. In my lifetime we have made huge progress in carving out better life chances and job prospects for ourselves. Much of this has come from forward thinking, engaged employers, but that would never have been possible without the powerful voices of employees with disability sharing their experiences. Everyone I have met has a very different story, but what unites all is a firm belief that there is a need for positive change. We all have a role to play in building disability confidence from the inside out.

This is our story.

CHAPTER ONE

Disability identity

When life takes a tumble

At first, there was no real indication of the seriousness of what was about to happen to me. I was 15 years old, just finishing my first year of studies for O levels at Longford Community School in Feltham, West London. The final hurdle of what felt like an intense three terms was a batch of end-of-year exams. Now they were done, dusted, marked and discussed, there were just a few more weeks of school and then the long summer holiday stretched out in front of me.

During the 'wind-down' weeks, we had been given a list of creative subjects to choose from and the one I'd chosen was macramé. I'd never tried it before. I liked the tangibility behind the tying of strange little knots. It certainly made a nice change from wading through textbooks to cram in all the revision from the previous months.

But after just a few weeks, I was aware that my wrists were beginning to ache. It was an odd sort of ache. It didn't feel like the sort of writer's cramp-style pain you get when you're furiously scribbling a three-page exam essay on *Macbeth*. This post-macramé pain was much more acute, and it didn't abate when I stretched out my arms. I was concerned but not worried.

The most likely explanation was that I had somehow pulled a muscle with my intensive knotting exertions, and I just needed to give my arms time to sort themselves out. Right then, the word 'arthritis' was a million miles from my mind. I was blissfully unaware that more than 350 million people have arthritis globally.[1] The World Health Organization (WHO) estimates that 23 million people around the world have rheumatoid arthritis (RA).[2]

As we inched towards the final day of term, I did my best to ignore the by-now constant pain in my wrists. It was difficult to do, not least because it seemed to be spreading up my arms. My head began to fill with all sorts of explanations about what it might be. None of them seemed particularly rational, but you'd be amazed at the sort of theories you can conjure up as to why something that had initially seemed so insignificant had begun spreading from my fingers to my toes. None of the theories were good.

Sharing personal information for the first time

Anyone who has experience of a new disability, whether it is overnight due to a dramatic accident, or a gradual onset of an auto-immune disease, will know how difficult it is to talk to others about your experience for the first time. Just saying the words out loud forces us to confront what has happened and address our fears of an uncertain future.

Obviously, this is not the same for everyone and many people will acquire their disability before birth, or during birth, or soon after. And this is an important point. 'Disability' is a term that covers many different experiences and levels of 'practice' in sharing personal information.

Whatever the situation or circumstance it is hard to say, 'I am scared.' I am scared I may not be able to work in the future. I am scared I may not live an independent life. I am scared I may not get married or have kids. The other side of this deep-seated concern is second-guessing how people will react. Will they think less of you? Will they look upon you as an inconvenience? Perhaps they may not even believe you. There is no real way of predicting how others will respond. You may have a hunch about who will be your fellow travellers on this journey, those who will take it in their stride, versus those who will be more concerned about what it means for them, rather than you. Or worse, that your experience is of no consequence. Whatever the reaction, you can never be sure it is the one you need.

'Disability' is a term that covers many different experiences and levels of 'practice' in sharing personal information

Getting all these doubts and fears right in your head is tough but speaking out about them at the same time seems an almost impossible mountain to climb. Therefore, many people live with uncertainty and fear about the future for a long time before they speak out.

I certainly fell into this bracket, keeping my inner anxiety to myself for many weeks. In fact, I didn't even mention at home that I was feeling any sort of discomfort at all. I told myself that I didn't want to worry my parents and in particular, Mum, who I knew would have become very anxious indeed. However, that was only going to last so long. The tenderness that seemed to drill into my very bones was making it hard to move around freely. Sooner or later, they were going to notice that their once active teenager was really struggling.

It was my mum, Barbara, who noticed first. On the second Friday morning of the school holiday, she'd encouraged me to accompany her to the shops. From the start, I trailed behind her on the pavement and could not keep up with her.

It was now clear I could no longer keep to myself what was happening. I told my parents that I was in pain, and it was just getting worse each day. I was consumed by a piercing, stabbing pain that left my joints feeling stiff and permanently uncomfortable.

My dad, Roy, received the information in a typically upbeat and reassuring way, telling me it was most likely some sort of bug that would be easily fixed. Time, or perhaps a prescription from the doctor, would sort it. It felt safe.

It was agreed that I'd be booked in for a check-up, as soon as the weekend was over, or a 'full MOT' as Dad called it. We were all going to a wedding that weekend and, as is so often the case with these things, there had been a big build-up.

We were due to leave early on Saturday morning. When I went to bed on the Friday evening, I was just supremely hopeful that the brief respite from pain that I felt most mornings would somehow see me through the whole day.

When I woke up, I knew straight away that something was wrong. Really wrong. The acute pain was there in greater force than ever. But, not only that, now I barely had the strength to move my limbs at all. I couldn't even raise my arms to lift the quilt. I felt pinned down by it.

'Mum, I really can't move,' I said as she entered the bedroom.

'What's the matter?' Mum coaxed.

I couldn't answer though. I watched helplessly as the enormity of the situation sank into my parent's minds. I hated worrying them. I never ever wanted to put the two most important people in my life through something like this.

'We need to call the doctor,' Dad said. 'We also need to call and say we can't make the wedding. Don't worry, they won't even notice we're not there,' he said. I doubted it and probably knew at that very moment, to share any information about your life is to unleash the assumptions of others.

Extra costs of disability

Weeks went by. Our local GP seemed to have taken up residence though seemed utterly mystified by my symptoms.

'There is a possibility of glandular fever,' he began. 'Or it could be a common-or-garden food intolerance. Alternatively, there's urticaria – a type of nettle rash,' he added. 'That would account for some of the raised rashes that we can see on the skin. We'd need to take some blood tests to be sure.'

'But they can all be treated?' Mum said.

'Once we know what we are dealing with, yes.'

It was probably just as well that, at that stage, I didn't know what was going to happen next. Or rather, not happen. As June stretched into July, then August, no one seemed able to come up with a definitive diagnosis. By September, the doctor was still no closer to working out what was wrong. As everyone returned to school to resume their studies, I was still a virtual recluse. While I didn't yet count myself as having a disability, I had learnt a brutal truth about how easy it was to drop out of your life, in this case school, largely unnoticed.

According to UNICEF there are nearly 240 million children with disabilities around the world.[3] The World Health Organization estimates that in some countries 'being disabled more than doubles the chance of never enrolling in school'. An estimated one in three out-of-school children have a disability.[4]

Life can cost £583 more on average a month if you have a disability

This has a knock-on effect on their life chances, meaning disabled children grow up to be poorer than other adults.[5] Scope, the disability equality charity, tells us that life can cost £583 more on average a month if you have a disability and families of disabled children face average extra costs of £581 a month.[6]

By this stage, my parents had moved my bed downstairs. Taking even one or two stairs was out of the question. There was a toilet on the same floor, so I could make my way there unaided, albeit slowly.

I remember being so conscious that my parents were spending more and more on me. Things like painkillers, a special diet with protein powders to help me put on weight, and creams to alleviate the rawness of my skin. I overheard them one evening talking about whether they had enough cash for Mum to take a taxi to the shops the next day because she wanted to get there and back faster without leaving me at home on my own. They didn't.

I remember even then thinking I would have to earn more money than the average when I grew up in order to undertake the most basic of functions. The pain I experienced meant I could not imagine using buses or trains, let alone ever walking again. These were the days when working from home/hybrid-working policies were decades away. The alternative to earning would be to live a more restrictive life. At 15 and without knowing what was happening, nor 'what I wanted to be when I grew up', I knew I needed to earn more to have a basic life.

Making sense of loss

My school was directly opposite my family home. I could hear the morning bell summoning pupils noisily flooding in through the gates. It was hard not to be affected by sounds of the ebb and flow of daily school life that seeped in through the window for the rest of the day.

Even my daily dose of morning TV couldn't mask the fact that it was a lonely and worrying time. As the weeks rolled into months, my best friend stopped coming. It really disturbed me. Maintaining any sort of friendship in a situation like this was all but impossible.

I worked out quite quickly that I needed to keep any negative thoughts to myself. I was disrupting family life. It was tough on my sister and brother to have my bed, with me in it, parked in the living room in front of the family TV. Sally was older at 17 so had a sense of what was happening. I needed some new clothes, so she went and bought a selection of perfect choices and there were some bargains in there too. Mum and Dad were running back and forth to the hospital to accompany me on endless appointments, taking time off work and dropping plans at a moment's notice. Everyone had to accommodate the almost daily disruption as we heard a succession of people say, 'I don't know.' They had no choice. It's just what families do when someone gets ill.

Resilience is rarely a decision

There are many things to learn when living with a newly acquired condition that gets in the way of how you'd have liked your life to pan out. It takes quiet thought. Part of this reflection time is so that you can begin creating your own practical work-arounds. And sometimes it is just grief about loss. In my case, it meant recognizing the possibility that my mobility was going to be deeply compromised by physical pain levels and fatigue. Even though there was no diagnosis in those first few months I already knew I had to accept that I was never going to grow up to be one of those women who juggles a career with motherhood, and be the life and soul of numerous social activities. I was going to have to make choices and compromises. I couldn't 'have it all'.

I was still young and confused about what was happening though I already sensed that I would need to prioritize the things that made me happy. Resilience is crucial. Navigating a new disability takes a lot of energy. I don't just mean in terms of not being able to do everything you are used to doing. It also takes all your reserves of strength to deal with other people. This was especially so when, without fanfare or warning, the formidable figure of the late Dr Barbara Ansell entered my life.

The first time I heard Dr Ansell's name was from my GP. In November, after months of confusion and uncertainty, he announced that had attended a lecture on paediatric rheumatology given by Dr Ansell, who was widely recognized as at the top her game when it came to joint disorders. Most specifically, she specialized in the research and treatment of juvenile idiopathic arthritis, or, as it was better known, Stills disease.

The doctor explained that Stills was a disorder that led to inflammation around the joints, and which is characterized by fevers, a salmon-coloured rash and arthritis. The other symptoms he described, such as those acute pains in my arms and legs, nausea, poor appetite and swollen lymph glands also sounded eerily familiar. It had typically taken a long time to diagnose for two reasons. First, while this was a disease that affected young people, hence the juvenile in its longer title, Stills tended to present itself in *very* young people who were, say, two or three years old, not well into their teens. The other reason was that it is notoriously difficult to diagnose in classic blood tests. Essentially, everyone had been looking the wrong way throughout all the blood tests I'd been taking.

Of course, the obvious next question was this: if it was indeed Stills disease, what could they do about it? More importantly: was there a cure?

I saw the doctor hesitate and knew the answer before he said it. No.

'It isn't yet possible, no,' the doctor began. 'Dr Ansell is doing a lot of work on it. The emphasis at the moment is to control the symptoms and slow down the course of the disease.'

This is how, towards the end of November I found myself heading back to Ashford Hospital in Middlesex for another battery of tests.

A lesson to learn: employers must earn trust

It would be some years later that I considered myself as having a disability. As anyone who has lobbied for or shaped and written legislation will attest, the complexity of defining disability in legislative terms (i.e. the 'definition' of disability for anti-discrimination purposes) is huge. Making sense of aspects of our identity and then sharing personal information about disability or ill health first requires you to have a good grip on how you feel about it yourself. Only when you have done that do you look for the clues that others will receive the information in a way you want it to land – and that includes our own view as to how trustworthy our employer is.

The complexity of defining disability in legislative terms is huge

In the 2021 briefing paper 'Five Trust Tests', PurpleSpace calls out the fact that while many employers will try to get accurate data about the number of employees with dis-abilities that they employ, they will forever fail.[7] This is partly because individuals must first make sense of a human experience that they would often largely prefer not to have. Then comes the struggle of sharing information with others because to do so is to let go of 'control' of how the facts may land, and what others may do with the knowledge. This is complex terrain. What is more, wherever an employer operates it is unlikely that they can simply rely on 'asking better questions' in order to get a better understanding of the impact of disability on their workforce and/or customer base.

John Amaechi, an organizational psychologist, calls it out:

> Workplaces fundamentally misunderstand disclosure – they think it's a means by which individuals tell workplaces (in this case) something less well known about themselves. However, telling your workplace you have a disability is less about you and ALL about your perception of your workplace's worthiness to learn about you. Your judgement that it has *earned* the right to know you better. Workplaces, and the leaders therein, must earn the trust of their colleagues.[8]

Practical actions for employers and employees

For employers

REVIEW YOUR EMPLOYEE ASSIST PROGRAMME

The employee assist programme (EAP) market has grown substantially in the last decade. In fact, in 2013 the first EAP Market Watch Report was published by the UK Employee Assistance Professionals Association.[9] The report cited how the market had grown by 69 per cent since 2008 and was then worth £69.13 million. That year, 23 of the 25 organizations listed in *The Sunday Times* 'Best Companies to Work For' report offered their employees an EAP. It estimated that half the UK workforce (at that time, 13.8 million people) were supported by an EAP.

It is worth noting, however, that most 'evidence' about the value of EAPs come from those with most to gain from the industry. For example, a later study in 2020 by the Employee Assistance Professionals Association, 'EAPs 2020: How does your organization compare?', suggested that for every £1 spent on an EAP, UK employers see an average return on investment of £7.27, whatever the size, company, sector, geographical location or service used.[10]

If your organization has an EAP it would be worth your while to assess how you review the skills of your EAP providers that purport to support your employees through disability/health challenges. At a minimum, ensure that during the procurement process you build in time to ask better questions of providers about how they help employees through transitions and trauma by connecting them with colleagues with similar experiences. Or you might ask how call-centre staff receive training about the internal workplace adjustment process. At a minimum get your own people with disabilities in on the review meetings.

DON'T JUST ASK BETTER QUESTIONS

When considering undertaking a monitoring exercise to determine how many employees with disabilities you employ, don't spend too much time worrying about creating the 'best' set of questions to ask. Asking 'better questions' alone will do nothing in your quest to create accurate data about the number of disabled employees you employ. You won't be able to. It is possible to ask 'better questions' but you will never have a true picture – so start action in other places (such as creating an easy-to-use, visible workplace adjustment/accommodation process with defined service level agreements).

For employees

DON'T OVER-THINK DATA MONITORING

Don't spend too much time over-thinking the intent behind data monitoring exercises of employers. Surveys are often created by well-meaning human resource professionals and diversity and inclusion managers who are ill equipped to understand the complexity of our lives. Data monitoring exercises are not drawn up to catch us out but to try and understand the number of people with disabilities our organizations employ in order to prioritize actions as part of their building a more inclusive working world. That is not to say that some of us will experience discrimination, but employers rarely start with that intent.

WRITE YOUR OWN STORY

Consider writing down your own story of disability/ill health – even for just your own private consumption. Ask yourself what you have learnt about yourself or others to plough that learning back to your employer in a way that can help create inclusive cultures and help allies support those that come behind us. If you have ever felt reticent in sharing your experiences, take comfort from knowing you are not alone. You are in a club of millions of individuals.

CHAPTER TWO

Nature, nurture and a new reality

Protecting others first

If you asked my friends to describe me today, they'd most likely say I am pathologically positive. Some of my good friends have used those very words. While I don't think my positivity is bordering on being a 'disease' I am conscious that there may be some personal cost to being relentlessly on the up. Though I can't help it: it's who I am and has largely served me well. Certainly, adjusting to the prospect of a lifelong disability required every ounce of positivity I could muster. It's a cliché to say we take our good health for granted until it is gone, but it is true.

The prospect of a lifelong disability required every ounce of positivity I could muster

If you were to trace my positive nature back, I think I inherited a great deal of it from my father. Roy Nash was the sort of person who always seemed to have a smile on his face. Even when he told a story of injustice, which was something that always infuriated him, he would do so with laughs along the way.

His own childhood was a challenge. He was one of eight children, born in Barnes, five years before the beginning of World War Two. When the war erupted, he was evacuated to live with his grandmother in Windsor. She was a fearsome character who scared the life out of her hugely extended family. Dad had lost both of his parents by the time he was 12. His father died from cancer during the war and his mother followed four years later after a failed gall bladder operation.

My mother Barbara was the eldest of three, born in Hackney, London, in 1939. She has always been eager to please and is so very kind, though struggled with anxiety all her life. I expect some of her anxiety stemmed back to her childhood. While she was initially evacuated to Nottingham during the Blitz in central London, along with her mum and younger sister, her mother quickly decided this was not for them and returned to the East End of London with her two girls. When Mum speaks of these times she mentions the horror of Doodlebugs, the V1 rockets that had rained relentlessly down on the East End. She talks too about how they could have been caught up with the Bethnal Green tube disaster on 3 March 1943, which killed 173 people who were crushed while attempting to enter the shelter. The fear of terrible things that can happen in our lives, as well as the traumatic events that do, can cause lifetime distress.

I am sure some of her vulnerability was in part, why, when I finally received my official diagnosis, I did my best not to share my sadness, to protect her as well as the rest of the family. When the doctor finally and solemnly announced that, yes, they now strongly believed it was rheumatoid arthritis, Stills disease, I remember glancing over at my mum, who was sitting at the side of my bed and I could see that she was crying. I was sad that she was crying though I knew then that I could not do the same. It would be years later that I realized that my sadness was not just because Mum was sad.

Now the diagnosis was official, I faced something that many millions before me have also experienced: I needed to fully make sense of my disability. Depending upon the condition, its severity and age of onset, a new disability can impact so much in your life. Thought needs to be given to every aspect of your future, from education, to employment, to interacting with family and friends, to financial circumstances.

In the mound of leaflets people are given, or websites we are directed to, there will be advice like 'give yourself time to mourn', or 'don't be tempted to put on a happy face'. Like many, I did the opposite, at least externally. I kept my fears away from others and with hindsight I think this was mostly because I was protecting others.

In retrospect, I see it is a pretty rubbish strategy, because you must still confront those fears, though for me it was years later when I was able to do that.

That said, even in the early days I gravitated to positive psychology to survive. I started reading about how people can learn how to reframe experiences. What could I learn from this? How can I help others in the future who may experience trauma? Might there be opportunities within the experience that could be shaped into a life that was fun and interesting and one where I could live independently?

All of this is often a lonely journey because we do not, at least in the early days, seek out the camaraderie and wise counsel that comes from other people with disabilities. Especially those who do not have the same impairment as us. We must reinvent ourselves first and often without great role models in our lives.

Dr Stephen Duckworth OBE broke his back at the age of 21 while playing rugby. He became paralysed in all four limbs. He speaks about how he:

> never enjoyed the privilege of going to school with disabled
> children, or playing with them in the park, or even travelling
> on the same bus. I had been segregated from them,
> marginalized and excluded. I lived in the rose-tinted world of
> severely able-bodied and brutally able-minded people.

It was Duckworth who first coined the expression 'I was the first disabled person I had ever met.'[1] He went on to create a very successful consultancy business to help organizations build disability-confident businesses. In that one expression he calls out the fact that disability, as a human experience, is light years away from anything assumed in our previous, sheltered and privileged non-disabled lives.

Cracking on

Things moved on surprisingly quickly after the diagnosis. One minute it was being confirmed that I was now among the 1,000 children per year who were diagnosed with Stills in the UK, and the next, arrangements were being made for me to go to the Canadian Red Cross Memorial Hospital in Taplow, Berkshire.[2] This was where Dr Barbara Ansell was doing her pioneering work. The idea was that I would go there for a few weeks for more tests and a fuller assessment and then, after Christmas, I would be admitted there for some months.

I arrived at the hospital in mid-December, for my first 'brief' stay. The hospital was housed in an imposing set of long, plain white buildings. The only part of the building that deserved the moniker 'grand' was the entrance, which was flanked by six huge pillars. I had been assigned to one of the three wards for youngsters with Stills disease. There was one for younger kids, one for teenage girls and one for teenage boys. Each ward was long and thin, sparsely decorated and punctuated with large picture windows. There were two rows of white metal hospital beds facing each other over a walkway between them. There must have been 20 beds per ward.

Some of the children had had arthritis for many years and many were wheelchair users. I'd never met, let alone lived, with disabled youngsters. I didn't want to stare but found myself doing so. Was this what was what was in store for me? It was the start of a lifelong journey in what it means to make sense of ill health and disability; to experience an uninvited change of identity.

My parents had to leave me there. That was the rule. It dawned on me that I needed to tough this one out on my own. No one could help me through this but myself. I managed a few days until I asked the matron if I could phone home. She relented and let me. My resolve completely crumbled. I sobbed down the phone, asking Mum and Dad to collect me. Anything had to be better than that place.

I remember Dad arriving the next day and he was alone.

'You're upsetting your mum,' he said, as kindly as possible. 'You need to stay here. The doctor says Dr Ansell is incredibly talented. She'll be able to help you. You need to give it a try.' I grew up fast.

While Dr Ansell was one of the most remarkable rheumatologists of her time, her treatment regime was based on keeping things moving. Left unchecked, Stills can cause irreparable, long-term damage to the joints, leaving them effectively fused for good. The treatment involved administering anti-inflammatory steroids to ease the swelling, and intense manipulation via physiotherapy to free up the limbs. No words can do justice to the sheer agony of what that 'intense manipulation' means.

Every Wednesday there was the weekly ward round after lunch. Dr Ansell was a large woman, in every sense, with an imposing presence.

Even though the ward visits were an ordeal, they were infinitely preferable to the treatments. We had to make our way to physiotherapy on the other side of the hospital. Walking was hard enough, but when you needed to make your way down hundreds of metres of gloomy corridors it was the worst sort of torture. The exercises were painful, and any sort of refusal was out of the question. This routine was repeated twice a day.

The only part of the day I looked forward to was being at school. This was a make-shift affair in a small separate out-building behind the children's wards. A rather eccentric 'teacher in chief' was Mrs Bolton. We called her Baggy Bolton behind her back. No amount of pain stops kids being kids.

Dealing with a new reality

It didn't take long to slip into the routine. Ward rounds, drugs, the agonizing walk to physio (times two) and then a short while at 'school'. And repeat.

The obvious reaction to reading an account like this is: how did we all survive? The answer is not very well in some cases. It is hard for any person to understand the onset of a disability in teenage, or indeed adult, life. Teens will inevitably feel a keen injustice, not just about the condition itself, but also about how it impacts their life prospects.

A teenager with any disability or chronic condition is at greater risk of depression than their peers

Young people resent the new-found restrictions on their freedom, yearning to live the 'normal' life of their peers.[3] It's not just Stills, either. A teenager with any disability or chronic condition is at greater risk of depression than their peers. To make matters worse, it can be harder to spot the symptoms because many of them overlap with the physical symptoms of disability, such as low energy and changes in eating and sleeping habits.

I didn't enjoy this new reality. I hated the fact I could no longer go to my old school and that my old life had changed forever. It's very easy to feel socially isolated. But

I remember looking at previous essays I had written, and homework done from a previous era. I could not believe the girl who had done those things did not exist any more.

Scenario scanning

I made a habit of scenario scanning, particularly when lying in my bed, late at night. At that stage, I couldn't walk any sort of distance, I couldn't dress myself and people had to cut up my food for me. I had to wear splints on my legs and wrists at night to keep them in place, so I didn't undo all the good work I had done in the physio room. The same questions just kept going over and over in my brain. What job could I possibly do? My sister was going through her university choices as she studied for her A levels, but neither of those avenues seemed open to me. It felt highly unlikely that I would ever return to mainstream school at all. If I ever got out of that hospital, would I ever be able to live independently? Would I have an apartment of my own? A husband? Children? None of these scenarios seemed immediately possible.

While many of my fellow patients there were depressed to one degree or another, I think we saved each other in a way. We were united in our worlds that provoked a certain amount of gallows humour. I found myself making some firm friends and, over time, I did start laughing. Often our situation felt so ridiculous, there seemed nothing else to do. Together, we rebelled in different ways. One of my best friends and I would sneak off, dodging the fierce ward sisters as best we could, so she could meet with one of the porters to chat in one of the side rooms. It felt pretty daring just to walk off the ward. Together, we would talk about hopes for the future.

Abuse of power

There was a serious side to our camaraderie too. We exchanged information on which nurses and doctors to trust and which ones to keep a close eye on.

'Steer clear of the optician,' one of my fellow patients said one day.

This was not necessarily an easy thing to do, since Stills can affect the eyesight, so we had to have regular tests. It turned out that this optician was not averse to copping a feel of a girl's breasts when they were taken for tests, particularly if she was a wheelchair user. As soon as the lights were switched off to begin the process, he'd lock the door and reach them from behind. As I look back, as an adult, I have raged. At the time, our struggles with disability, pain and mobility took precedence. And our stories and laughter helped us through.

Thirty years later I had dinner with an 'old inmate' friend. She reminded me of the optician, and I shared with her that I hadn't experienced what she had. We had been at the hospital at different times, so I mused that perhaps he was a different optician. 'Or maybe your boobs weren't as good as mine,' she quipped. The rest of the evening was a right-off, we could not speak for laughter. Sometimes human beings cannot fight too many battles at the same time. We had to choose how to survive first. She died a few years after we met for dinner though her deliberate and conscious use of humour to make sense of difficult experiences lives with me. She did not belittle her experiences; she confronted them.

One evening, just a week or two before I was discharged, I remember listening to the newly released track *Breakfast in America* by Supertramp. It was 1979. My heart skipped a beat. There was something deeply hopeful and moving in the lyrics. It was a playful, jubilant song, reminding us of the 'myths' we might tell ourselves about a 'promised land', in this case, America. Equally, though, it could be referring to the myth of not having a disability or experiencing ill health. The upbeat tune goads us to be happy with what we've got, because what we imagine others have is not always a heavenly place. I knew I had to play the long game because life could get better.

Despite the few small, good moments I was eager to get out of there as soon as I could. Dr Ansell's work was pioneering at the time because she worked towards a position where the progression of the disease could be slowed down or burnt out. The steroids that were used to get us to this stage were strong, and had side effects, but for the time being it was a huge breakthrough. I should add that things have progressed a lot further today. Young people with Stills are treated as day patients now and can benefit from modern 'disease modifying' treatments. Fewer people will experience the progression of the disease that my contemporaries did and, even if they are diagnosed as toddlers, the outcomes are more promising in terms of less joint damage.

At the time though, all that I had to bank on was the fact that I needed to be one of the ones where the inflammatory disease was kept at bay and/or burnt out.

By June 1979, six months after I had arrived at the Canadian Red Cross Memorial Hospital, I was told I could leave. I was far from well and it was clear I would have to live with arthritis my whole life, though it is hard to describe the feeling of elation that I felt when I was given the news.

When Dad arrived, the chief physiotherapist talked him through my exercise regime.

'It's imperative that Kate does this at least twice a day. If you don't, Kate's ability to walk will be compromised.' Dad listened and nodded and made all the right noises.

It wasn't long after we had set off on the drive home when Dad pulled in from the road outside a newsagent shop. He came out with a big bar of Bournville chocolate and plopped it in my lap. 'Don't tell the others,' he said, with a wink.

A lesson to learn: workplace adjustments/ accommodations are neither music nor chocolate

Listening to music and eating chocolate are two of life's simple 'gifts' when you are at your lowest. The upbeat tune from *Breakfast in America* and an 'illegal' bar of chocolate from my dad, made tough times slightly nicer.

The first incident was an impromptu reminder that life can be lovely again because music (or any art for that matter) can often capture ironic truths about human experiences that come from other people's assumptions such as politicians, welfare rights workers, doctors, social workers or employers.

The second was a naughty spontaneous act of love from someone who couldn't 'fix this stuff' for me, but who could make life a little nicer, even fleetingly, as I stuffed the chocolate in my mouth as part of a secret pact.

Both seemingly insignificant moments, though it is interesting I have the sharpest recall of their impact over 40 years later. They helped develop a degree of resilience from other peoples' stuff and a lifelong habit of searching out the positive moments in life.

My point being that workplace adjustments/accommodations are neither music nor chocolate. They are neither insignificant moments nor happy accidents. They are not to be begged for. They are not 'gifts' to be earned by deserving people with disabilities. They are a necessary duty that employers are legally required to make in order not to discriminate against employees with disabilities.

The Convention on the Rights of Persons with Disabilities (CRPD) was adopted on 13 December 2006 at the United Nations Headquarters in New York. The Convention was negotiated during eight sessions of an Ad Hoc Committee of the General Assembly from 2002 to 2006, making it the fastest negotiated human rights treaty. As of 5 January 2022, there are 185 countries that have signed and ratified the fact that it requires them to implement law that makes reasonable accommodations a legal obligation.[4]

Workplace adjustments are our lifeline

Workplace adjustments are our lifeline. If your workplace adjustment/accommodation process isn't as visible and as easy to activate and deliver as your maternity leave process, you are failing your employees with disabilities.

One of our members said during one of our personal development courses:

> How come, as a woman I feel supremely entitled to my maternity leave benefits. All I do is give my employer 15 weeks' notice. The rest just happens. As a disabled woman, I tie myself in knots just gearing up to ask for the most negligible of adjustments. As a woman, I feel worthy. As a disabled woman, I feel a burden.

Practical actions for employers and employees

For employers

AUDIT YOUR WORKPLACE

Wherever you work it is always worth conducting a root and branch audit of your workplace adjustment/accommodation process. In addition, appointing a board director to understand what is working well, and what is not working as well as overseeing the outcomes, is vital. Be prepared to invest, in the knowledge you are likely to be saving money in the long term.

Certainly, consider too the need to centralize both the budget and the process by which your people can secure workplace adjustments/accommodations. At a minimum create a toolkit or 'knowledge repository' for your people about the very many easy, low-cost ways in which your organization can offer a workplace adjustment. It can be as cheap as an easy-grip pen.

CONSIDER SERVICE LEVEL AGREEMENTS

Undertake a review into the length of time it takes your organization to deliver an adjustment/accommodation to someone – especially those adjustments/accommodations that require a piece of kit, or some accessible software or an ergonomic mouse. Ask further questions about whether your organization has agreed and published service level agreements with timelines by which they need to deliver an adjustment/accommodation and build in a routine review to ensure they are still relevant and working effectively. Ask yourself: if your organization does not have service level agreements, why it is OK for women to expect the maternity policy to kick in at a certain point in time (because babies do not wait. Mostly). And then ask yourself why it is OK for timelines to be sometimes ill defined and protracted for employees with disabilities.

The largest ever award payout of £4.7 million was made in 2020 when a UK bank was deemed to have failed to make the adjustments required for one of its workers. This type of payout is rare. Tribunal awards for disability discrimination between 2019 and 2020 averaged £27,043 while the medium was only £13,000. With the average cost of adjustments being between £450 and £700 it seems sensible to ensure the process is visible, easy to use and seamless.

For employees

DO YOUR OWN RESEARCH

Do your own research about the myriad of workplace adjustments/accommodations that exist. They include 'hard adjustments/accommodations' such as an ergonomic mouse or a software package to enable your computer to read out words if you cannot see them on a screen. And they include 'soft adjustments/accommodations' such as being able to finish earlier on a particular day so you can access one of the talking therapies that help you manage your mental ill-health experience. We may want our employer to just 'know' about these things and all the ways by which the workplace can be accommodated/ adjusted for people with different disabilities. However, in my experience, they do not always know. I wish it was different too.

REMEMBER YOU ARE WORTH IT

Get a large mirror that belongs to you alone. Every day stand in front of it and repeat 'I am worth it.' If mirrors are superfluous to requirements imagine yourself standing in front of you as you say these words. Asking for the things that others take for granted can often be one of the most difficult aspects of our lives. There is no quick way to get used to this and it is possible that you will forever find it hard. Having now lived with disability for nearly 45 years I still find it hard to ask others to do things for me or a bit differently around me. But I do. And I am so worth it.

CHAPTER THREE

The soft bigotry of low expectation

Planning for a life less rosy

Somewhere along the line, when I was at the Canadian Red Cross Memorial Hospital in 1978, I got it into my head that I would be dead by the age of 60. Having been on large dosages of very strong steroids I assumed this might have a long-term impact on my health and lifespan. It meant that I didn't want to hang around: I was keen and eager to get on with my life and make up for a year's lost time.

There were no disabled role models at that time at all. No one spoke about their experience of disability. When you watched TV, there was never ever a disabled character in a drama or in the news. There was no such thing as a disabled celebrity in films. It was as though 650 million people from around the globe didn't really exist. If you looked hard you might occasionally read a story in the newspapers about a person with a disability. You might catch wind of the odd stories about wheelchair users being removed from cafes or cinemas for 'taking up too much space'. Or, of a visually impaired woman being turned away from a restaurant because she wasn't allowed in with her guide dog.

Physical access to public services was patchy. If I did get a job, how would I get to work each day? I was ambulant at that point, but that could change again. Wheelchair users needed to give three days' notice to travel by train and were then offered the 'luxury' option of being seated in the guard's van.

In different parts of the world, quota schemes were starting to pop up and none of them were the same, which requires the need to question the validity on which they are based. For example, in the Disabled Persons (Employment) Act of 1944 in the UK, a quota system had been introduced requiring employers with 20 or more employees to ensure that at least 3 per cent of their workforce were employees with disability.

In Germany all employers with a workforce of 20 or more are required to fill 5 per cent of their jobs with severely disabled employees. In France the law requires that companies having a total workforce of more than 20 employees must ensure that at least 6 per cent of their personnel are disabled workers. There were all sorts of mixed messages coming from large employers. Certainly, there were many businesses that completely failed to make facilities available which might encourage a more diverse workforce and requirement to make adjustments/accommodations. And it was often the case that employers would prefer to pay the fine or penalty for non-compliance rather than make the effort to build an inclusive workplace.

The most prevalent messages around disability at the time centred around philanthropy and charity with all the sadness, pity and low expectation that comes with it. This soft bigotry of low expectation of others was a curse. To sum up the worldwide them-and-us, arms-length view of disability, the United Nations designated 1981 'The International Year *for* The Disabled'. Any cries of dissent that 'surely it should be *of*', to indicate that the community was fully on board and part of the celebration, were apparently ignored. Surprisingly enough, people with disability played little or no role in the key events.

Skills are skills, irrespective of disability

High on the list of my priorities was financial independence. I wanted a career. I knew that for certain. Certainly, Mum and Dad had always encouraged their three children to do well at school. They wanted us to go to university and prepare for what came next. Times had changed since my Mum had had to abruptly end her aspirations of a career in fashion in order to bring up her young family.

High on the list of my priorities was financial independence

I was able to narrow my choices, by a process of elimination. I decided very early on that maths and science were not for me. Fortunately, my antipathy towards these subjects was matched by my love of reading. I never had my sister's writing skills, but I loved books and the stories of others.

Anything that touched on what makes us humans tick was fascinating to me. It encouraged me to broaden my reading into sociology and psychology. I wanted to understand why people said one thing when they meant another, how we organized ourselves, what subtle gestures said about us and all the other millions of nuances that go into making us human.

When it came to choosing my A level subjects, it was Mum who played a big part in helping me consolidate what to do. She had a cleaning job at our school and was assigned to the classroom devoted to sociology. She'd looked at the various posters on the walls and some of the books scattered around the desks and thought: *Kate would like this*. I had barely heard of sociology when she mentioned it. I had a look into it though and it seemed to fit the bill.

Identify and invest in natural allies

I was nervous walking into the sixth form centre on the first day back at school. Being in hospital put me a year behind. I had to make new friends. It was a big change for everyone in the year, moving from the main school to the more relaxed, 'grown-up' atmosphere of the A level years, though everyone seemed to taking it in their stride. It wasn't just the fact that I looked different and moved differently than everyone else that really made my stomach churn though. I knew it would be hard to keep up the pace of getting round the school.

Each lesson began the same. I'd arrive in the class and sit down for the lesson but would only ever be notionally listening. The thought that would dominate was how I would tolerate the pain to get from that classroom to the next one for the following lesson. I barely heard a word. I was planning how to stand up without other people staring.

My school life changed a lot for the better when I met Karen Prince-Wright who quickly became one of my best friends. Karen was head girl. She was kind, popular, sporty and very outgoing with a tremendous sense of justice. She'd spot something that was not right, or something that needed to be done and she'd just do it. She was never concerned with the optics. She did what was necessary.

I remember the moment when we had to begin formulating our Personal Statements which would support our university applications. The school kept emphasizing how important it was that we were shown to be well-rounded human beings.

'Universities want more than just great grades,' the head of the sixth form had said. 'They need to see evidence of your character too. What do you do outside school? Do you play on a sporting team? Do you have a Saturday job? Have you been volunteering? These are all essential components of your Personal Statements.'

I closed my eyes and sighed. It was difficult not to feel at an instant disadvantage. I did very little outside school, other than attend medical appointments.

I was sitting in the sixth form common room when I became aware that Karen was standing in front of me.

'Hi Kate,' she said with a smile. 'Glad I caught you. I've made you Vice Head of House Neptune. You'll need to collect the registers from the tutors at the beginning of the day and take them to the school office,' she said.

She must have seen the look of horror on my face as the enormity of what she'd said sunk into my brain. Those registers were enormous. Great big, hard-backed, A3 books. There was no way I could carry even a few of them from classroom to classroom.

It was then that I understood a new challenge brought about by my arthritis. I would have to practise the art of saying, 'No, I can't do that. I am not physically able to make that happen.' I needed to find a way to articulate it in a way that protected and preserved my dignity, while at the same time not causing offence to the person who had made the request. It was going to be hard to say things to people who were entirely unfamiliar with what I'd been going through. I already knew this wouldn't be a one-off too. This would be my reality for the rest of my life.

'I can't do that,' I said finally.

Karen didn't blink, she asked, 'Why?' So I was completely straight with her. I explained that I had been diagnosed with arthritis at the end of the previous year and there were things I found very difficult to do. Getting around was one of these things, which meant the whole register thing was not a goer.

'Ok,' Karen nodded. 'I'll get someone else to do that bit.'

I didn't know it then, but at a stroke, Karen had put into action a part of what would eventually become a key feature of anti-discrimination employment law in different countries many years later: the duty to make a 'reasonable adjustment/accommodation'. This is the legal phrase used to describe the changes employers need to make to ensure disabled people receive what they need to help them do their job as well as someone who is not disabled. Karen had, instinctively, just put it straight into action.

Karen had given me a gift. She hadn't only extended the hand of friendship and given me a meaningful role in the sixth form. Suddenly, I had something interesting to put about myself on my Personal Statement. I was part of the leadership team of House Neptune. I was beyond grateful.

I learnt a lot about myself as well as the role of allies. I realized that there was absolutely no need for me to be deeply apologetic about my disability, just as there was no need for her to make a great deal about it all the time. It was just as it was. There was no big fuss. No overly concerned enquiry of 'Are you feeling OK, Kate?' No awkwardness or embarrassment. Just an invitation to the crowd to play a game of poker.

Karen's activities outside school were infamous too, particularly her parties which I always felt a part of. I couldn't dance but I never felt left out. I'd sit on the sofa, with my glass of wine and I'd watch it all. The evenings invariably ending with some elaborate group dance sequence, and it would always be hysterical to watch. Friends, cousins – we were all insiders. Their re-enactment of *I will survive* by Gloria Gaynor was a riot to watch. It is right up there with *Breakfast in America* in terms of long-term impact. Uplifting but with a twist of hysteria.

Navigating pity

I still needed to get my place at university and that felt a challenge. It would likely mean me living independently and I couldn't envisage that.

One afternoon, I was sitting at the kitchen table. To distract myself, I began to look at the classified job ads in the newspaper. *What jobs were there that didn't need a degree? What could I be when I grew up?* Mum, who had spotted what I was doing, interrupted my thoughts.

'Kate, it would be fantastic if, one day, you could get a little job,' she said encouragingly.

Except I didn't hear the encouraging words from my ever-supportive mother or recognize that she only ever had my best interests at heart. All I heard was the word *little*. As in, insignificant, inconsequential, irrelevant or, let's face it, pointless. A little job.

My mother had, albeit inadvertently, summarized the challenge I now faced. Packed into that seemingly inconsequential word 'little' were a whole host of themes and implications. For a start, it was telling me that there were always going to be physical issues in the way. This was years before equalities legislation for people with disability, so my choice of career would most likely be limited by the facilities offered by employers.

Then there were also going to be cultural, behavioural and attitudinal issues to grapple with; in other words, what people thought of me. I would face an uphill battle to be accepted for who I was, however clever or talented I was. I lived in a world where people could still tell me, bluntly, to my face that they could not employ me because

I was not physically up to the job. Again, there were no laws to stop this happening. I'd grown up with stories of hotels and landlords putting up notices saying things such as 'no blacks and no Irish'. While abhorrent and outlawed, I

I would face an uphill battle to be accepted, however clever or talented I was

faced a similar sort of blanket discrimination. *No disabled allowed!*

Perhaps the most profound implication of Mum's statement was the realization that if I did not find a way to preserve and protect my 'brand' and source the techniques and personal behaviours to work my way around other people's lack of expectations for me, it would have a significant deleterious impact on my career and prospects, as well as my own mental health and well-being.

The aspect of that conversation that had the biggest impact on me though, was the fact that the words had been spoken by my Mum. She was someone who cared for me deeply. She'd made sacrifices for me since the moment I'd been born and has continued to do so without complaint or question ever since, even in the most challenging of circumstances (at 83 she still does, for each of her three children). She wasn't coming from a position of hate, or prejudice. Yet, her statement about the little job was her best take on my circumstance. *One day, you could get a little job.* If that came from a place of love, what do you do with that? Pity is soft and insidious. It can come with love and care and that is what makes it really hard to navigate – and at work, more than anywhere else.

I do not blame my Mum for her words. They fuelled me and I thank her. Such words helped me, and many more thousands who also experience such reactions (and still do) to spot the 'well-meaning' human responses, yet inadvertent discrimination, where (entirely wrong) assumptions are made on our behalf. Human beings are a broadly compassionate breed. Unfortunately, because we can't live or feel every experience, we tend to 'fill in the blanks' with our imaginations. Or we feel overwhelming disappointment, or sadness, on another's behalf and act on these often-misguided assumptions. Where it becomes most corrosive though, is where people reduce their expectations of what might be possible for another person. As I discovered that day, compassion can often go too far.

What I had to do now was to decide whether I was prepared to allow that soft bigotry of low expectation to thwart my ambitions (although it came from a position of love), or was I going to head it off at the pass? That was a big question for a teenager to answer.

Aiming high

Something changed in me that day. Then and there I resolved that I wouldn't just get into university, I would go on to get a first job and then a bigger second job and then a positively towering, important and consequential job, which would, in turn, broaden out to become a meaningful career. And more than anything I knew I would do something significant before the end of my life.

I didn't know it then, but I was giving myself what modern organizations now call 'stretch goals'. These are not just challenging goals. They are the equivalent of moon shots, in other words, goals that seem unattainable given the current situation, available tools and capabilities. To be this radical requires a new approach, to find ways to bring these goals within reach. Working hard is a given but working differently is key. There may need to be some sort of intervention, certainly a cultural change and that needed to be backed by legislation. Meanwhile though, I would need to build on my reserves of personal courage while I did all of that. Right then though, I had no idea how I would go beyond any little job I may get. I just knew that I would.

A lesson to learn: we must turn conflict into positive experiences

In his book *The Power of Difference*, Simon Fanshawe shares a story about when he was an impressionable teenager reading RD Laing.[1] He reminds us that RD Laing's own son thought it ironic that his father was a well-known psychiatrist when in the meantime he had very little to do with his own family – he was an alcoholic and experienced depression.

Fanshawe found RD Laing's work bleak:

There was something, on the face of it, very disheartening about his assertion that 'I cannot experience your experience. You cannot experience my experience. We are both invisible men.'[2]

Fanshawe goes on:

> I found the whole sentiment thoroughly dispiriting until
> I caught on that it was the attempt to understand each
> other's experiences that yielded the richness. He was just
> stating our profound separateness. Once we all recognize
> that, then we've got a journey to go on together. The truth
> about humans is that maybe the only thing that we have in
> common is that we are all completely different. And we can
> never properly know one another. ... To seek to understand
> each other's differences is an essential human challenge.
> To know that we never will is the human condition.

Fanshawe also talks about his early experiences of listening to his parents argue about money. He says he 'inherited an emotional landscape from my parents in which life is lived through the conflict of opposites'. He goes on to recall that it was only when he was in his forties, and when starting to meet people who accepted that conflict is a given, that he realized that sometimes, against every expectation, managing conflict can produce remarkable and optimistic results. He reminds us that conflict comes in many forms: 'casual rudeness, language that offends, relationships that damage us, and friends or family who turn their back on us'.

He concludes, 'In one way or another it will always feature in our lives, so the question is how will we respond? What choices will we make?'

Fanshawe went on to be the co-founder of Stonewall. His work has had a profound impact on global corporations and many hundreds of thousands of people and their allies. What strikes me as important is his fearless ability to look inward as an integral and essential part of the process of looking outward and managing conflict and discrimination.

For me, dealing with the inward conflict I face from the inadequate remarks of others is still my responsibility first and foremost and requires an active and positive response. I have learnt that never goes away, despite all the legislation or line manager training that exists (or doesn't). I don't excuse the inadequacy of others that comes from lack of experience or curiosity or their over-reliance on assumptions. And I certainly don't consider my personal actions to manage conflict as 'fixing' myself, but I profoundly believe that my life is enhanced and made richer much more by the actions I take (or do not take) than by micro-managing the education and lack of training of others who have less experience of disability.

Practical actions for employers and employees

For employers

FIND ALLIES

Consider encouraging your employer to set up an ally programme at work. They are growing fast in the business community and offer a great practical way of getting non-disabled colleagues to feel helpful and useful in the process of building an accessible working world.

Benny Higgins was CEO of Tesco Bank, with 500,000 employees, for 10 years. He was known for highlighting the value of ally programmes, especially in the LGBT+

community. As a heavyweight in the financial services sector, he always emphasized the need to build inclusive workplaces as a necessary part of building profitable businesses. Before he left the bank, he had already been suggesting that ally programmes were now required for people with disabilities:

> The expression 'straight ally' has become an important part of the lexicon in the LGBT community… But the notion should be important in all communities seeking to protect and progress their interests and identity. Indeed, I favour the unqualified use of 'ally' because it says everything we need to know. An ally of the purple community is someone who promotes support in some way. It is someone who recognizes that those with a disability play a crucial role in our society – no less important than any other. Allies can make a difference. And we can all be allies.[3]

Similarly, Martin Taylor, Combat Air Director of BAE Systems, calls out the fact that working in industries that may pose more challenges for people with disabilities does not excuse inaction. 'Engineering and manufacturing environments can pose challenges around accessibility, but it is our job as leaders to remove barriers, make all our workplaces accessible and attract diverse talent.' He concludes, 'The role of disability champions and allies is crucial in bringing about a cultural shift towards greater inclusivity.'[4]

Working in industries that pose more challenges for people with disabilities does not excuse inaction

During his time as Global Head of Diversity and Inclusion at Barclays Bank, Mark McLane often spoke of the power of allies:

> Creating an inclusive and welcoming environment is vital to enabling colleagues to bring their whole selves to work, to bring difference to the table and know that it matters. At Barclays we have seen the power of allies in building such a culture, for example our Male Allies support gender equality in the workplace. We launched Reach Purple Champions as allies to help us create a workplace that is disability and mental health confident.[5]

RESEARCH REVERSE MENTORING SCHEMES

Research as many examples of reverse mentoring schemes as you can and consider introducing one at work if your employer hasn't yet got one. These are schemes where you link people with disabilities (the mentor) with people who would like to learn more about the lived experience of people with disabilities (the mentee).

These are not new techniques. It was Jack Welch, the former CEO of General Electric, who popularized reverse mentoring in 1999 when he required 500 of his top executives to pair up with junior associates for the purpose of learning how to use the internet.

CMS Energy Corporation and its principal subsidiary, Consumers Energy Company, is Michigan's largest electric and natural gas utility, serving 6.8 million of the state's 10 million residents. It has 9,500 co-workers and offers eight employee resource groups (ERGs) to help foster an environment where all employees feel they belong.[6]

Their employee resource groups operate a reverse mentoring programme where all officers at the company are paired with someone within the company from a different demographic for a year-long mentor/mentee relationship. Employees mentor the officers in the programme, and if an officer is paired with a member from capABLE, the Disability ERG, they may have the opportunity to learn from a person living with a disability.[7]

Similarly, global law firm Freshfields Bruckhaus Deringer has a reverse mentoring programme, Diverse Perspectives, which connects junior and mid-level colleagues who identify with belonging to an underrepresented group within the firm with a senior colleague. Many of the junior mentors are members of the firm's affinity networks including Freshfields Enabled, their disability network. The mentoring scheme is open to all colleagues in every office across the firm and in 2021 their programme featured 52 pairs from 16 offices across the globe.

Says Reena Parmar, senior knowledge lawyer and Enabled Network Co-chair, 'Understanding, being compassionate about, and engaging in dialogue about disability and accessibility can vastly change our and our colleagues' day-to-day working experiences.'[8]

For employees

IGNORE HOLLYWOOD'S VIEW

Lift yourself out of reading all the Dis-Mis-information about our lives. It will seriously impede your ability to think clearly about the myriad of ways it is possible to secure employment and/or live independently. This is a hugely important part of staying positive in the quest for your first job or indeed throughout your career. And it's not all about the data and statistics that purport that we are not in work or that employers don't want our skills. Our story is still not adequality expressed on screen or stage either.

In her book *Being Heumann: The unrepentant memoir of a disability rights activist* Judy Heumann, one of the most influential disability rights activists this century, calls out the irony between how our lives pan out, and how the world frames our experience.

'Sometimes Hollywood tries to tell our story,' she says:

> You've seen the movie. A woman acquires a disability, and wants to die, and then convinces a loved one to kill her. *Million Dollar Baby*. A man acquires a disability, wants to die, but then falls in love with his personal attendant. To 'save' her from a lifetime with a disabled man he kills himself. *Me Before You*. A man acquires a disability and turns villainous in the face of the agony. *Star Wars'* Darth Vader.

She makes her point with unrelenting examples:

> Disability is seen as a burden, a tragedy. But what if it wasn't? What if someone's story began with the words: 'I never wished I didn't have a disability.'[9]

INVEST IN YOURSELF

Invest in your own personal development. Do it consciously and conspicuously and as generously as you can afford, and online accessibility allows. It can have a real impact on your work and your life chances. It could involve you watching one TEDx Talk on YouTube each week.[10] It might include you investing in your access to the Blinkest online application to receive concise summaries of great reads and podcasts that will fuel you towards your goals.[11] Or it might be about signing up to Masterclass, the online library of classes that enables members to learn from artists, leaders and icons around the world.[12]

Investing in yourself is about how you spend your time. I totally get it that our time is often spent in battling with the stuff that gets us to a level playing field. But with what is left, think about how you can invest your time to nourish your belief that bright days exist.

CHAPTER FOUR

Who do I want to be when I grow up?

Basic practical choices

In October 1982, I found myself at Froebel College, which was part of the University of Roehampton in southwest London, signed up to study sociology and social administration. It hadn't been my first choice. I had originally been interviewed at the University of Kent in Canterbury and by the University of East Anglia. However, fate stepped in, and I didn't get the grades I needed. So I applied to Froebel College and my sister came along with me to the interview. She voiced both of our thoughts when we walked through the grounds, she said that it was perfect.

'You can really get around the college and it is close enough for Dad to come and collect you if you need anything.' As ever it was the practical and pragmatic viewpoint that led my available options.

University was a real highlight. I felt accepted as the person I was when people met me. I met some incredible friends who are still an important part of my friendship circle. If we went out, they would look out for the right chair at the right height for me. Or if drunk after a night out, they'd drag my boots off.

I left Roehampton with an OK degree after three amazing years. I watched friends fall in and out of love, date good guys and wild guys, get engaged, get married. Hours of midnight discussions about love and life. Finding love wasn't high on my agenda, though my head was turned once at the infamous Froebel Summer Ball by a man (let's call him Richard) who went on to do great things. Mum had made me a beautiful blue velvet figure-hugging cock-tail dress. I matched it with blue lace gloves to disguise my fingers. A wonderful shop assistant at John Lewis depart-ment store helped me try on what felt like hundreds of pairs of gloves to get the right fit on my misshapen hands. Some memories remain etched in your mind for a lifetime. I remember Richard reading from a poster on my college room wall which recited the poem *If* by Rudyard Kipling.[1] We giggled at the sexist nature of the last line: 'You'll be a Man, my son!' I liked it that he questioned things. All things.

When he left my room, I kept rereading the Kipling poem. It offers a set of rules for grown-up living. I used to read the poem every day, several times a day. It urges you to keep going, keep going, keep going. It kept me going.

My time at Froebel helped banish a lot of the negative thoughts about 'belonging' in an important friendship circle and being able to live independently. When I left Froebel, I first secured a summer job at Reading University, teaching English to Italian students. My sister was doing the same and had managed to get me a job too. Dad would drive us from Feltham to Uxbridge each morning. The three of us would sing *Johnny Come Home* by Fine Young Cannibals at the top of our voices as we rode in his white Citroen 2CV. Life felt it was taking off.

Trying to find role models

My initial thoughts on preferences for my first job were quite broad and were marked by dismissing things that I knew I could not do. I'd have loved to do something in design and dressmaking, following in the footsteps of my mum, but there was no chance I could do that. One must be dextrous to do dressmaking. This meant focusing on other skills and gifts.

In my spare time, I sought out books about disability, though there wasn't much. It was hugely important to me to understand other peoples' experiences. So much literature at that time, and indeed still today, is mere 'inspiration porn', and pumps out messages of triumphing over adversity. This did not hold any interest.

There were no political texts about disability at that time. I'd grown up in the seventies, a time which had seen the introduction of the Race Relations Act and the Sex Discrimination Act, which were designed to protect people against discrimination on the grounds of their race or gender. But there was very little about the real experience of disability.

It would be some years later that you could find anything meaningful about the societal construct of disability such as the *Politics of Disablement* by Mike Oliver or *Pride*

Against Prejudice by Jenny Morris.[2,3] The conversational and accessible work of Tom Shakespeare in *Disability: The basics* was decades away.[4]

There was one book around that time that stood out for me. It was an autobiographical work called a *A Disjointed Life* written in 1980 by Corbet Woodall who had been an actor as well as an English newsreader for the BBC.[5] His book recounted his 14-year struggle with rheumatoid arthritis, and he wrote the book to help medical professionals to understand the mental and emotional aspects of the condition. In an article for the Arthritis and Rheumatism Council magazine giving his reasons for writing the book he wrote:

> However brilliant and affective the surgeon or rheumatologist may be, it cannot be easy for them to understand the purely personal, and sometimes very difficult, problems which they necessarily create for the patient afterwards. Nor do I believe, by the way, that it is part of their job to do so. Heaven knows they perform enough miracles on our bodies without having to do that same thing with our minds when it is all over.

The book made me ill at ease, though I agreed with his sentiment. I remember reading two years later in 1982 he had died quietly in his sleep aged 53.

Supporting others to live independently

My first experience of the workplace didn't bode well for my future career aspirations. I had secured a job at a hospital which operated as an institution for adults with learning difficulties. The hospital complex was spread over several wings of austere-looking, imposing brick-built buildings. The word 'incarcerated' sprang to my mind and it was hard to find it anything but chilling.

The job I'd secured was to assist the team of psychologists. The team was tasked with teaching the adult residents the essential skills they needed to help them transition from the hospital into the community. Many of the residents had profound learning difficulties, which meant it could be quite challenging for them to undertake simple tasks, whether it was making a cup of tea, to learning how to shop or use a bus. Three adults were in my charge. The plan was that I would teach them enough skills to enable them to move into a halfway house, where they would live independently. At that stage, such an idea was groundbreaking and it was in great part why I had chosen to take the job. Helping people to get away from institutionalized care by supporting their development of life skills was something I was strongly in favour of.

Feeling the weight of the underclass

By far the biggest challenge for me was working with the attitudes of many other staff. There was just far too much gossip couched in very demeaning and disrespectful terms.

The biggest challenge was the attitudes of many other staff

One day I walked into the staff room and overheard a lively conversation about which resident was 'shagging' another resident. I was horrified they felt it was acceptable to belittle people with learning difficulties.

We were a long way from affording people of difference the dignity and respect they were due.

As it happened, I had an opportunity to exit. I had, occasionally, visited an adult day-care centre in Kingston and was offered a job there. The job itself was quite like the one I was doing at the time, except it was focused on teaching skills in a day-care rather than a residential setting.

Just before I resigned from my job I was completely poleaxed by a sudden and extremely painful flare-up of my arthritis. I was plunged back into the same level of pain and discomfort that I had experienced when I was 15 years old and first unable to get out of bed. It was an unexpected and extremely unwelcome repeat visitor to my life. I had to go back home to live.

Managing a fluctuating condition

In many respects, the adult training centre was a far better environment for me. The job was nine till five, without shifts, and I really enjoyed the work. The main challenge though was getting there. It was a two-hour round trip each day using buses and walking from bus stops. It was just too physical. I began to become worried about another flare-up, returning me to square one and back to my bed.

I didn't know it, but my hips were beginning to wear out. This is not an uncommon occurrence with inflammatory arthritis. I had to leave my job after only a year. I had never wanted to do a desk job, but this was looking increasingly like the only option that might be open to me. Anything physical was just too taxing.

I had to sign on as unemployed. If I was in any doubt of my new-found, reduced status as a registered disabled person, I was also given a card, which confirmed it. It was hard to be optimistic in the face of these developments. I'd had two cracks at the workplace and neither had worked out as I'd wanted.

Initially, I felt a little numbed by it all and cut off from the world. I felt a new wave of loneliness. My experience is not uncommon. While people with physical disabilities often struggle with mental ill health, the predominant reaction is to supress any negative thoughts. This is in part because there is a much more immediate need, which is how to move around and get things done, which is something that most people take for granted. Worrying about our mental health always seems like a bit of a luxury. Would I have been better off if I had been given some support in this direction and been encouraged to discuss how I felt? Would I have been less brittle? I guess I will never know. Certainly, as time went on, I found myself becoming increasingly adept at dismissing my feelings.

As I thought about potential jobs for the future Mum got into the habit of bringing in the Wednesday society job ads section from the UK's *Guardian* newspaper, to see if she could tempt me to apply for something.

I suspected my next move would be something to do with 'people' though I didn't really know where I might focus.

A lesson to learn: you have to look back to make sense of things while living forward

In her book *Driving Forwards*, Sophie Morgan, the television presenter most known for her lead coverage of the Paralympic Games on Channel 4, looks back over her life.[6] At 18 she had a life-changing injury following a car crash. She details the long road of rehabilitation:

> As the weeks turned into months, visitors came to see me less and less, my friends had jobs to do or university to attend…
> I didn't want to be too needy. I had even asked people not to 'waste their time' visiting me.

She reminds me of someone.

Sophie did much of the hard graft required to bang on the doors of fashion and retail companies to encourage them to tap into the largest untapped market in the world. She set up a consultancy company and drew up some ideas. She had a product manufactured: a wheelchair for a mannequin. She had success and a major retailer's flagship store in Central London installed her prop in the window display.

But she also recalls that with every step forward there were many steps back and doors slammed in her face. While courting one company she accidently received an email from someone who had mistakenly copied her into their reply to someone else: 'We will always be "seen" to support disability, but we won't ever do it in our windows', they say. 'Please someone, get rid of her.'

Sophie retreats for a while though muses, 'You can't just "get rid" of people like me.'

I am reminded of the film *Pretty Woman* and the bit when Julia Roberts returns to the store that hadn't wanted to take her custom to taunt them with the line 'big mistake', her arms full of shopping bags carrying the most expensive items of up-class products. That will be you, Sophie. Of that, I have no doubt.

Practical actions for employers and employees

For employers

EMPHASIZE THE BUSINESS BENEFITS

Equip yourself with a detailed analysis of what you might be missing out on if your organization does not take account of disabled customers. Learn from companies who are themselves out, loud and proud in their wish to tap into the purple market.

In the ILO report `Making the future of work inclusive of people with disabilities' it is reported that $1.2 trillion was the annual disposable income of disabled people in 2019 alone.[7] Whether this is about the physical shopping experience or indeed the online experience, examine the examples of businesses that are leading the march. What is clear is that both high-street and high-end brands are now starting to shine a spotlight on people with disabilities. Italian *Vogue*, in partnership with Gucci, ran an editorial beauty shoot featuring Ellie Goldstein, an

> *$1.2 trillion was the annual disposable income of disabled people in 2019 alone*

18-year-old British model diagnosed with Down's syndrome. The images generated one of the brand's most successful ever Instagram posts, with more than 865,000 likes.

In the last five years or so we have seen a rise in the number of disabled social influencers who have hundreds of thousands of followers and who are now being courted by big brands to help sell products. And we are seeing some brands adapting their product line to ensure their products are accessible. Tommy Hilfiger offers the Tommy Adaptive range of clothing, their goal being to make getting dressed easier for everyone. In 2021 Proctor and Gamble (P&G) adapted their Herbal Essences Hair Care product bottles to include tactile bottle markers. It can be hard for visually impaired consumers to identify products while in the bath or shower where sight aids are not typically used.

It is of no surprise that the mastermind behind the move by P&G came from one of their own visually impaired colleagues Sumaira (Sam) Latif. Sam talks about her own personal struggles with products which fuelled her desire to fix problems for people with disabilities. She says:

> Now that I was a mum, I used many of our products, some with ease and others with much difficulty. I could never independently read my Clear Blue pregnancy test result, had a challenge reading the size of the Pampers diaper, differentiating between the Olay day and night cream, Herbal Essences shampoo and conditioners. I began evaluating our products in terms of accessibility. I had recently switched from using Ariel liquid detergent to Ariel Pods and found the transition amazing as I no longer was having challenges with measuring out or spilling the

liquid detergent as I could just pop a pod into the washing machine. We touch five billion consumers around the world and 20 per cent of these consumers will have some form of disability like me.[8]

It is of no surprise to me that Sam has been an influential leader in the global growth of their disability network. The People With Disabilities (PWD) Network was created 38 years ago at P&G when the United States enacted the Americans with Disabilities Act. Sam expanded it into Europe in 2014 and then started to lead the network globally in 2017. Learning directly from their own people has been an important strategy to build their accessible product range.

ADOPT A ZERO-TOLERANCE APPROACH

Take a zero-tolerance approach to colleagues who use derogatory terms or demeaning remarks to describe disabled customers, potential suppliers or consultants or indeed users of your services. Imagine the person who sent that accidental email to Sophie had been referring to gender:

> We will always be 'seen' to support women, but we won't ever do it in our windows.

Imagine the follow-up remark being said by a man:

> Please someone, get rid of her.

If you take a zero-tolerance approach to such abuse, ensure you help all your people understand the personal consequences of not adhering to such policies. It is fortunate that Sophie had the verve to come back after such brutal remarks. Many don't. In my mid-twenties, after my first hip replacement, I remember going to my local hospital for rehabilitation in a hydro pool. When I was hoisted out of the water and walked back to the dressing room to get changed I overheard two middle aged staff talking. 'She has such a beautiful face,' said one. 'Just a shame about her legs and hands,' said the other.

For employees

READ OTHERS' STORIES

We all learn in different ways. Some of us like to read books. Others will surf the net and prefer podcasts and short soundbites. Whatever your 'thing', ensure you soak up the broadest range of literature that exists and that is written by those who have 'trod the boards' when it comes to personally navigating disability, ill health, accidents or injury. We hear this expression about actors who put in the hours learning their trade acting on the stage. It sums up the emergence of a new dialogue comprised of people with disabilities who are now prepared to share their stories. Whether the stories are from political activists with a big 'P' in front of the word 'political' or those individuals who see themselves as a differently 'shaped' change agent. Some stories you will love. Some you will hate. Some will make you gasp at how much they mirror yours.

PLAY THE LONG GAME

Whether that is about getting your first job. Or the next job. Or whether it is about having to balance your time and your energy in advance of seeking any job at all. I love every aspect of Rudyard Kipling's poem *If*. I especially love the line, 'If neither foes nor loving friends can hurt you.' Of course, like the rest of us, I have been hurt by both, but it doesn't stop me from ensuring I keep practising the art of not allowing other people's 'stuff' to destroy my enthusiasm and energy.

CHAPTER FIVE

Disability is a political experience

Disability has always been political

I'd had a keen interest in politics for as long as I could remember. I had never seen myself getting into the frontline of politics. While I applauded the democratic process, I knew it had its flaws. At the residential home I'd worked in I'd witnessed the impact of policies which were formed without real insights into the people who would be subject to them.

Politics still fascinated me though. I enjoyed the legislative process, seeing how initial ideas become policy. Importantly, legislation creates 'have tos', in terms of how societies organize themselves, prioritize spend and treat people. Yet it can never stop there. It is and should always be about what comes next and how we make things better.

I wanted to contribute to this process, from the outside. I was fascinated by stories where one person has the capacity to set new directions. I loved reading about figures such as Gandhi, Nelson Mandela or Mother Teresa, who each in their own way changed the course of history. The story of Rosa Parks haunted me: with one simple act in refusing to move from the 'coloured section' of a bus, she had such impact on the US Black rights movement. I was not presuming to put myself in the same bracket as these historical figures, but I enjoyed the idea that one person can make big changes.

I realized my efforts needed to focus on the way we approach disability. The legislative system was behind the curve in comparison with the progress relating to sex or race anti-discrimination laws. It seemed that disabled people were increasingly being left behind – there was no widespread will to change though the argument for anti-discrimination legislation was starting to be mooted. There needed to be much more collective pressure.

These thoughts were the clue as to why the job ad for a campaign researcher at the UK charity Spastics Society (now 'Scope') caught my attention. The campaign's central aim was to equip parliamentarians with evidence for a Bill that would bring in much-needed protections for disabled people. The job description was about disability, campaigning for change and being strategic at a political level. I knew these things would lead me in the right direction.

There was a small problem with my masterplan. The job was way above my expertise level. The salary alone told me that: it was more than three times what I had received in my last job. Plus, the parts of the job description listed pointed to a range of skills I didn't yet have. It was, without a doubt, a very senior position. Yet it was one of the most exciting prospects I had ever seen.

Unable to help myself, I wrote requesting further information. A short while later, a large envelope was pushed through the letterbox. As I read the information I 'felt' my future. Even so, I couldn't get away from the fact that I was still wildly under-qualified.

In the end, I decided to write to the Head of Campaigns & Policy at the Spastics Society, Amanda Jordan, and lay my cards out on the table.

'I don't have the skillset for this position, and know you can't consider my application,' I wrote, 'but I would like to offer my services on a voluntary basis. Perhaps I could assist whoever was appointed to do this important job?'

I knew that there wasn't a chance in hell that I would even make the interview stage if anyone matched my CV against the job spec. If I could convince them to take me on as a volunteer, it would be a really good way of getting my foot in the door. It's very difficult to be too hard on someone who is offering her services for free.

Judicious use of sarcasm goes a long way

By this time, I had been in and around the workplace long enough to know that the interview process for people with a disability is not kind. These were the pre-legislation years with next to zero barriers on what could be asked at interview; this was often taken as carte blanche to ask pretty much any question, however intrusive, personal or downright

The interview process for people with a disability is not kind

impertinent. That's not to mention that most of these questions had nothing to do with the ability of a person to do the job. My mind kept going back to my interview for the adult training centre a year or so earlier. Out of nowhere, in the middle of the process, one of the interviewers had posed an extraordinary question.

'What would you do if, when walking down the corridor, someone with challenging behaviour issues attacked you from behind?'

For a few moments, I was stunned. Why were they asking me this? It was such an incredibly loaded question. Subtext: you clearly are not physically able to withstand such an event. Yet, what would *any woman* do? She'd do her best to wriggle free and call for help. This sort of loaded question was not a one-off experience either. When I went for my interview with the residential home I'd been asked pointedly what I *couldn't* do. Just to drive the point home, the interviewer 'helpfully' threw in a few examples. 'Are you, for example, able to change a lightbulb?' he said.

I was bemused. Dozens of answers flashed through my brain. There are so many things I cannot do. How to answer! *Well, I can't speak Chinese Mandarin. I can't scuba dive. I don't think I would be much good walking a tight-rope come to think of it.* My list of 'can'ts' may have been longer than the average person, but that didn't for one moment mean I couldn't do the job. I felt wrong-footed by a question designed to wheedle out candidates, but with an apparent scant regard for how they might feel about such an arbitrary selection criterion.

I was not alone in experiencing this blatant discrimination. At that time, people like me were routinely subjected to some of the most excruciating and naive questions in an interview setting every single day. It is not easy to bat away the ignorance with a witty repost, or the judicious use of sarcasm. You can't tell the person who asked it to get stuffed either, because clearly you are trying to impress them and land the job. It's a really nasty Catch 22. No wonder the prospect of interviews terrified me. I had no idea what sort of intrusive question I'd be asked next: 'So, Kate, do you really think that you'd be capable of captaining the next lunar mission?' 'But, er, isn't this a job managing an Earth-based lobbying campaign?'

Creative ways to give someone a break

When I did finally meet Amanda, I felt like I had died and gone to heaven. She was mesmerizingly clever and kind in equal measure. While she and I were under no illusions, I was offering to work for free after all, so it was all upside for her, she responded to me as an individual. She was very evidently interested in me. She wanted to know what it was that made me passionate about campaigning. What did I think could be achieved? What did I know about the current situation? Why did I want to change the world?

My meeting with Amanda was like a breath of fresh air. Instead of relentlessly focusing on my weaknesses, here was someone who only wanted to hear about my strengths. When she'd finished this rigorous series of questions, Amanda was clearly satisfied with my responses because she seamlessly moved onto talking about a piece of research that was being done on making polling booths more accessible for the impending 1987 general election. Then, as indeed is still the case today, many voting centres were housed in church halls, schools and village centres. At the time, many of these venues were completely inaccessible to many voters, particularly wheelchair users. It was also rare to have additional

Here was someone who only wanted to hear about my strengths

facilities such as hearing loops, which again made the whole process inaccessible for a whole section of the community.

'Would you be interested in assisting the research director by doing some interviews with disabled people about their experiences trying to vote?' she asked.

I said yes straight away.

Amanda concluded by saying they would be able to pay for my tube fare to travel to and from the office each day and give me an expense allowance for lunch. I was thrilled. It might not sound much to anyone reading this today, knowing I was giving my time for free, but to me, at that moment, it was a gift. The opportunity to volunteer and work for a campaign that might conclude with anti-discrimination legislation was more than I could ever have hoped for. And I didn't have to stand for most of the day.

During my time I helped on two or three out of what was eventually to be 11 private members bills that the Spastics Society and importantly many other organizations of disabled people were involved with. This was a period that really marked the beginnings of the momentum towards the Disability Discrimination Act (DDA) in 1995 and a number of British politicians were emerging as huge supporters. Exeter MP John Hannam, Lord Ashley of Stoke, and political campaigner and then councillor Roger Berry emerged as passionate champions of disability and human rights. Not everyone demonstrated such openness to progress though. This meant it was a hard slog and, for every step of progress made, acres of evidence needed to be presented in order to persuade, cajole and convince members of parliament across all parties. Organizations such as the Spastics Society knew that one of the best ways to effect change was to build relationships with MPs. Many of these MPs only had enough budget to employ part-time researchers so they were very receptive to anyone who offered to help and gather the large amounts of information they needed. Particularly so if they offered to do it for free. By doing so, it made the politicians much more receptive to the campaigning messages we were building on our own behalf to serve our membership and wider community.

On Tuesday afternoons, I would sometimes go to the House of Commons for the All-Party Parliamentary Group for Disability. I revelled in working for an organization that encouraged you to go and listen to parliamentary debates and then report back on them. While there, I was starting to meet influential campaigners such as Ann McFarlane, Rachel Hurst, Jane Campbell and Stephen Bradshaw. For a time, I supported the secretariat for the Voluntary Organizations for Anti-Discrimination Legislation (VOADL) which had been set up in 1985. This committee was significant in the struggle for equal rights for people with a disability in the UK because it signified a decisive coming together of organizations of disabled people, such as the British Council of Disabled People

(BCODP), along with the more traditional organizations for people with disability like the Spastics Society and the Royal Association for Disability and Rehabilitation (RADAR). The group's sole purpose was getting anti-discrimination legislation onto the statute books. I didn't know it then, but each one of these organizations was to have a big impact on my outlook and career even though it was a fractious time with much in-fighting. Whenever the meeting took place at our offices, I remember digs and remarks about non-disabled people making assumptions about our lives.

When these meetings took place at our offices it was my job to help people back to the reception area for them to be able to leave. After one particularly challenging meeting I was in a lift with two of the visitors. Both were electric wheelchair users. Both 'big names' in the campaign. I tingled with excitement. I asked if I could help press the button to the right floor as I wasn't sure they could be reached from a seated position. One replied, 'Haven't you heard anything that was said in there about you lot making assumptions about our lives?' I was shocked and bruised and wondered whether key people advocating legislation would make 'room' for people with unseen disabilities in the legislation. Or indeed room for people with unseen disabilities to be part of the campaign to lobby for legislation.

I had no prior experience as a researcher or a lobbyist and learnt a great deal from Amanda Jordan and her team. They were masterful lobbyists of politicians. It felt like I had, at long last, found my true calling. This was something that stretched me, both mentally and physically and I was learning every day. I learnt about early day motions, and white papers and green papers. I learnt how to get good (discreet) information from civil servants who knew the landscape and wanted to do what they could for a cause that mattered. You never hear about the extraordinary faceless civil servants who do what they can, within the rules, to make it easier for lobbyists to secure good data. I learnt how members of parliament worked, how there was a definite good cop/bad cop routine in Westminster and that the whole thing was wrapped up in a great deal of hugely dramatic theatre, the likes of which you could pay a fortune to see on a Broadway stage. But, away from the drama and all the posturing, progress did seem to be being made.

Health-wise, my arthritis was not on my side during this period. I was fine for the first few months, but as time wore on, I began to be in a lot of pain. It was becoming increasingly obvious that I would need a hip replacement. In the meantime, my Dad, as always, did his bit to help out. He'd drop me at the tube station each morning, to spare me the bus and the walk. I had found what I wanted to do and loved every minute of the job. It wasn't just the job either. Working in Central London was exciting. I didn't have much money, but it seemed like I was in the middle of things. Part of where it was all happening. Life was wonderful.

The benefits of volunteering

I had also embarked upon a second degree. I wanted to futureproof myself, so whenever I got in front of an interview panel in the future, the decision about employing me would be an absolute no-brainer. I'd be the best qualified person in the room: no lightbulb-changing skills required. Therefore, I'd signed up for a Health and Illness Master of Science (MSc) at Southbank University, which meant attending classes on Tuesday and Thursday evenings, after work. I was walking with a stick. I'd grab a taxi outside the Spastic Society's office to Southbank University and Mum and Dad would drive into Central London to pick me up after I finished my lectures. Moving around the university itself was not easy, particularly when I was in a lot of pain and there seemed to be endless flights of stairs.

The course I took was designed to help practitioners such as occupational therapists to make the workplace better for people with a disability, or those who have recently experienced an injury or accident that changes their situation. These were the days before adjustments/accommodations were legal obligations. I couldn't help noticing though that, while the course had the right motivations at heart, it was somewhat steeped in the old language of rehabilitation and resettlement.

After six months of volunteering, I secured a full-time job as a research assistant at the Spastics Society. It was a new position meaning there was not a vast salary to go with it. The best they could do was offer me £6,000 per annum salary. I was delighted: the happy culmination of my original plan in stepping forward to volunteer. The problem was, now I had a full-time job, my paid-for travel and lunch expenses ended. That would have been fine for those who could use the tube, except my hips were starting to be so painful I needed a taxi to get into Central London and back. That would have cost me £125 a week. The maths suggested my weekly travel bill came to the same as my wage after taxes were taken out.

My colleagues swung into action and encouraged me to apply for Access to Work: a scheme that granted access to a non-means-tested benefit that helped with the costs of getting to work, or any equipment you might need. The scheme was administered by Disabled Resettlement Officers (DROs). I applied, but even before I knew the outcome (I was successful), I made the conscious choice that even if my whole salary was swallowed up by my travel costs, I would carry on. The job was important to me: I knew it would move me into the field where I needed to be.

My rage against my wonderful mum's remark about a 'little job' could abate. I could see the possibility of a 'big job'. And while my new £6,000 per annum job was not going to get any accusations of fat-cat-style salaries any time soon, I started to feel that my future could be of my making.

A lesson to learn: volunteering programmes and internships are underrated

It is not hard to find research that espouses the benefits of volunteering. Especially on the value for the business sector in driving employee engagement. In 2011 Deloitte published its 'Volunteer IMPACT Survey' which was commissioned to explore the connection between work-place volunteerism activities and employee engagement.

They used indicators such as workplace satisfaction, pride and loyalty and compared the responses of Millennials who frequently volunteer against those who infrequently or never volunteer.

They conclude that Millennials who frequently participate in workplace volunteer activities are more likely to be proud, loyal and satisfied employees, as compared to those who rarely or never volunteer. They discovered that Millennial employees who frequently participate in their company's volunteer activities are:

- twice as likely to rate their corporate culture as very positive, as compared to Millennials who rarely or never volunteer (56 per cent versus 28 per cent)
- more likely to be very proud to work for their company (55 per cent versus 36 per cent)

It is much harder to find research on the value that volunteering offers disabled individuals to get their first break, though you often hear it directly from disabled people themselves. In a podcast with Samantha Renke, actor, presenter, speaker and disability rights campaigner, she talks about the significant role that volunteering played in her capacity to launch her career.[1] When asked about how she has got where she has, she says, 'By saying yes to everything and then figuring out how the heck to do it when you're there.

Unemployed people who volunteered were roughly 7 per cent more likely to have found employment one year later

In an article in *Forbes* in 2013, 'Proof that volunteering pays off for job hunters', the author cites 'Volunteering as a pathway to employment', a study conducted by the Corporation for National and Community Service, a US federal agency that promotes volunteerism.[2,3] The researchers tracked more than 70,000 jobless people between 2002 and 2012 and found that those who volunteered had a 27 per cent better chance of finding a job than those who didn't. In another study 'Does it pay to volunteer?: The relationship between volunteer work and paid work' it was found that unemployed people who volunteered between 20 and 99 hours during the year were roughly 7 per cent more likely to have found employment one year later compared to those who didn't volunteer.[4]

Practical actions for employers and those looking for work

For employers

TRAIN YOUR RECRUITERS

Ensure you include adjustment/accommodation knowledge in your recruiters' basic skills training. This is not disability awareness training or unconscious bias training flimflam. This is training about the myriad practical ways an employer might adjust the working environment for people with different disabilities. What recruiters need is often practical knowledge about the types of adjustment that can be made by the very organization they work for.

CONSIDER STUDENT PLACEMENTS

At the same time, make sure you consider the creative introduction of student placements, paid and non-paid internships as well as other work experience programmes. I am not advocating you substitute critical staff roles with free labour. On the contrary. However, it is clear to me that had I not received a welcome 'yes' all those years ago from Amanda Jordan to my offer to work for free, in the trade I knew I had to enter, I may never had secured the break I needed. Be generous with the opportunities you have to change the working landscape for others.

For those looking for work

LEARN ABOUT THE POLITICS

Identity politics is the phrase often used to describe a political approach wherein people of a particular gender, religion, race, social background or class, environmental or other identifying factors, develop political agendas that are based upon these identities. There is no doubt it has played an important role in advancing civil rights, though notoriously fraught with controversy. Politics doesn't float everyone's boat though reading about and watching films about the politics of change, when it comes to the experiences of people with disabilities, can be a powerful tool to gain perspective on the challenges we can face, and the painfully slow road to change. It is worth doing the homework to learn about the road to legislation.

In 2020 Netflix released the film *Crip Camp*, the first documentary of its kind. It tells the story of a groundbreaking summer camp for teens with disabilities which proves to be such an important time for the people who take part that they go on to help build a movement for change, and their connection and camaraderie ignite their journey to activism and adulthood. It is of no surprise that those most known for campaigning for the Americans with Disabilities Act 1990, such as Judith Heumann and James LeBrecht, experienced the summer camp.

Two years later in 2022 the BBC released *Then Barbara Met Alan*, a television drama film based on the story of real-life couple Barbara Lisicki and Alan Holdsworth, the founders of DAN, a disability activism group. Written by Jack Thorne and Genevieve Barr it charts the contribution direct action had, as part of a range of important contributions, that led to the Disability Discrimination Act in the UK in 1995.

I expect we will see more such films in the future. I predict that it will be the Sam Latifs and the many other strategically placed disabled influencers in business that will create the next step change in designing more accessible working worlds and products and making manifest the legislation that was so hard fought for.

TAKE UP A VOLUNTARY POSITION
Strongly consider taking a voluntary position. Seriously. If there is a trade you want to get into, and there are no openings, or you are worried about knockbacks or lack of experience, then consider offering yourself for free for a time in order to get on the ladder.

CHAPTER SIX

Build your network to get ahead

Another interesting interview!

I spent two years at the Spastics Society, six months voluntary and eighteen months paid. Then an opportunity came my way via one of the lecturers at South Bank University. The Arthritis Care charity was recruiting a director for its 35-Group subsidiary: a network of 75 young people with arthritis, from all over the UK. These individuals, or 'Contacts' as they were known, ran self-help groups within their geographic areas. They organized meetings, talked to those who were newly diagnosed and helped them to source any necessary support given the often-considerable gaps in what Social Services could offer. They also offered encouragement for anyone feeling low or vulnerable, a service that can't be underestimated. The 35 in the group's title referred to the fact that the Contacts were all under 35 years old.

I knew I had to apply. It would offer the opportunity to run services, albeit voluntary services, at an operational level. And I knew I could incorporate my desire for anti-discrimination legislation by corralling evidence about our lives and offering it to my colleague lobbyists. And I loved the idea of this breathtaking army of young individuals who, like me, had had arthritis in their early years and were working hard to pay it forward. They were me. I was them. The job couldn't have been more different from my previous one though: it would involve travelling the length and breadth of the UK. To be effective, I knew I'd need to get in front of them at least once a year. By this time, I'd had my hip replacement operation and the pain relief had been almost instantaneous. I was still walking on crutches, but I was much more mobile than I had been for months. I loved the idea of being part of a 'tribe'.

I applied and was invited to an interview with Jean Gaffin, the healthcare luminary along with one of the senior Contacts. Thanks to two years at the Spastics Society I was hopeful things might go a bit more smoothly at interview. I figured that if any organization was to understand the needs of a young person with arthritis, this had to be it. As it turned out, the interview was tough. Jean eyed my crutches and asked how long it had taken to walk again. I told her it has been six weeks before I had walked properly again. I saw a flicker of doubt.

'Well, of course, we are very busy here,' she said quietly, though out loud. 'We really couldn't afford to have anyone off for long.'

She, like many other employers, was simply struggling to understand what they might do if, after employing someone, they then had to take large periods of time out. Luckily, she was just voicing her own fear – she did not let it, for one moment, get in the way of her decision. I got the job and Jean became an important mentor and advocate for young people with arthritis. She was outspoken, feisty and always set the highest standards of work.

Surfacing the names of famous people with lived experience of disability

Shortly after I arrived, I led the rebrand of the 35-Group to become Young Arthritis Care. There were three staff in total who worked out of Arthritis Care HQ in Central London, and there were 70+ volunteers, or Contacts, around the country. They were passionate, committed individuals who wanted to make the world a better place for young people with arthritis. I needed to be sure that they felt connected with me and with one another.

I got into a routine of travelling. I'd drive to the Contacts based in England and Wales, take the train for those in Scotland and would fly to Northern Ireland. I'd spend a few hours with each volunteer, and we would talk about the best way of offering advice and support to young people struggling with a new diagnosis. Once a year, we'd congregate in London for the Contacts' conference to discuss how we could better deliver for young people and we ran personal development courses for young people with arthritis.

I was also responsible for delivering a quarterly magazine. When I arrived, the original newsletter had been parochial with stories of hospital fêtes and recipes. I rebranded and repositioned it to make it into a harder-hitting magazine with useful and informative articles that offered insights and hope.

This was conveyed through the regular interviews with people who had positive life experiences with arthritis and/or who had done something amazing with their careers. We wanted to show that most of us could have a purposeful career if we wanted one. I got to meet and talk to personalities such as Brian Redhead from Radio 4's *Today* programme, as well as writers, including Roald Dahl and Rosemary Sutcliff. Years previously Sutcliff had perhaps the biggest impact on me when I read her book, *Blue Remembered Hills*. The author had also been diagnosed with Stills disease as a child and had gone on to write children's literature and historical fiction. I had the thrilling opportunity to travel to her house in Sussex and meet her. Before we met, I reread her autobiography and was even more struck by it. The focus of my attention was a couple of paragraphs. To anyone else they were of the blink of an eye: easy to miss. They were about the novelist being in love. He didn't share her love and she didn't pursue it. At that point, she knew that her life would not be characterized by a significant love interest, and she would concentrate on her writing. This troubled me. It continued to trouble me throughout the interview with the author, who was alone in her plush home, bar her attentive staff. It was a rare moment of negative reflection for me. I remember being pleased when the taxi arrived to take me back to the train station.

I still experienced severe loneliness on a personal level. Oddly, what I didn't know then was that I had recently set in train a series of events that would see me married within a few years.

The social model of disability without denying human need

I had not long since returned from the first International Youth Congress for young people with arthritis which was held in the Netherlands in 1989. At the end of the event, which had had such a buzz about it, I couldn't help myself but announce that the UK would be delighted to be the next host! Of course, then I had to go back to Jean and face the music for my very public commitment without any mandate. We had what you might call a 'challenging conversation', but as ever Jean's passion for justice came through and she said, 'OK, let's get it done. We don't have the budget for next year, maybe the year after.'

Three years later in 1992, we hosted the second International Youth Congress Meeting, and listening to the stories of the young people around Europe and the UK with arthritis brought everything that I had been doing up until this point into sharp relief. I heard story, after story, after story of young individuals who were blocked from the workplace because of their disability. One told me a harrowing story of blatant and entirely unnecessary discrimination: this had a devastating impact on her life chances and mental health causing her to consider ending her life. After leaving school, she had applied for countless jobs, but had been knocked back time and time again. Eventually, completely discouraged, she'd given up trying to get into the workplace altogether and had never had a job. The reason that her story really affected me was because there were so many similarities between us. We were the same age and had both acquired late onset juvenile arthritis at the same time. When we met, it was as though we'd known each other for years. We talked about how it was when we were 15 and our lives changed, almost overnight. Yet, after that, we followed very different paths and my progress had been fuelled by anger. That is tiring and not the experience of most, who can end up feeling crushed.

But she was not alone in her experience. A similar story was repeated everywhere I went. One man from Sweden lost his job because his employer refused to make any sort of adjustments whatsoever to accommodate his recent diagnosis of mild arthritis. All the skills and experience he had acquired from years of working for this same employer counted for nothing. Since it was not a legal requirement for his employer to make an adjustment, they saw no imperative to do so.

No one was helping the business community to get excited by this untapped talent market

All he would have needed was the opportunity to work one day at home. No further cost and no loss of productivity. It was lunacy to see so many people's potential buried under the weight of employer assumptions.

What economic arguments will never show is the personal stories behind the individuals who lost their jobs. It didn't matter how often I heard the accounts from individuals who had become unemployed as a result of arthritis (and I heard a lot), they always brought me up short. Pushing people out of the workplace caused an immeasurable amount of distress. It was deeply demoralizing too, because the people who lost jobs knew that they could do them with just a little bit of support and understanding. It didn't help that one of the peculiarities of arthritis is that it can ebb and flow. Some days you can walk confidently into a building. Other days you will be poleaxed with pain. While the good days are always great, they add to the latent stress around the experience of fluctuating conditions: about not being believed and, as a result, quickly dismissed.

As I started to look more deeply into the employment situation for people with disability, I thought back to my work experiences when I had been pointed in the direction of the job centre Disabled Resettlement Officer (DRO). While mine had been helpful, the feedback was that they could be a bit of a mixed bag. Inaction on the part of the DROs didn't exactly encourage change among employers. Quite the reverse. And even more importantly there was no one helping the business community to get excited by this untapped talent market. The DROs were never going to cut it. To be a great advocate of people you must, after all, really believe in the talent you are trying to place.

Securing employment was a lottery for people with a disability. You may get a broad-minded, welcoming employer, who was willing to make adjustments/accommodations. Or you might not. Unfortunately, the latter scenario was the most common. This was the moment when I began to really recognize that my contribution needed to zero-in on the employer's community at a very practical level.

Securing employment was a lottery for people with a disability

Playing a part in the disability movement

My time at Arthritis Care offered an opportunity to start working with the growing band of disability rights protagonists in the UK and globally. These were the individuals, with direct experience of disability, who were leading the movement for change and working hard to get the disability discrimination law in place. I was introduced to several game changers, such as the late Caroline Gooding, a lawyer, and the late Bert Massie (later Sir Bert Massie) at RADAR, as well as his colleagues Agnes Fletcher and Victoria Scott.

There were some big names associated with the growing movement for change and, as I got to know these sometimes larger-than-life characters, I could see many parallels between their stories and mine. Jane Campbell (who years later was made Baroness Campbell, thanks to her pioneering work) had been diagnosed with spinal muscular atrophy at the age of one and her parents had been warned that she would not live beyond the age of two. She survived and was sent to a segregated school for disabled children, where academic achievement was not high on the list of priorities and she left with no qualifications. She gained an MA at the University of Sussex, with, fittingly, a dissertation on the tireless campaigner Sylvia Pankhurst. Jane had been a forthright campaigner herself ever since. Then there was Rachel Hurst CBE who lost her teaching job aged 30 after becoming paralysed. She was later diagnosed with congenital myopathy. She started the Greenwich Association of Disabled People and Centre for Independent Living and became chair of the British Council of Disabled

People. She eventually helped set up Disability Awareness in Action, an international information network on disability and human rights. Mike Oliver, who had used a wheelchair since breaking his neck in 1962 in an accident while on holiday, was a passionate advocate of the 'social model of disability', a phrase he himself coined. This is the idea that a great deal of the experience of living with a disability is not directly linked with the disability itself, but rather a failure of society to adapt and meet the needs of disabled people.

There were splits among campaigners, often based largely on questioning the values and motives of those who worked for organizations 'of' or 'for' disabled people. Organizations *of* disabled people were part of the governing instrument. These organizations had rules which said X per cent of trustees need to be people with disability, or there need to be an X per cent disabled representation on the payroll. Their policies were predicated on the lived experiences of people with disability and were often structured as centres for independent living. They also tended to be more grass roots and much more led by disabled people. Charitable organizations that were called *for* disabled people, on the other hand, such as the Spastics Society, Leonard Cheshire, Royal Association for Deaf People, were often far bigger and far better resourced. The 'of' side rightly questioned the strategic intent of the larger not-for-profits. They were seen as too philanthropic and too cosy. Mostly, they simply mirrored societal perceptions in general.

Identifying your brand and delivering well

While I was in the 'for' camp, by dint of the fact that I worked for Arthritis Care, I was also working directly within a department 'of' disabled people at Young Arthritis Care. And over a period, I worked under two 'revolutionary' chief executives who worked restlessly to ensure the organization's policies were led by people with arthritis. There were always arguments about speed of change. But I saw it happen and was proud to work with senior allies who had a strong sense of justice and were thick-skinned enough to keep going if their motives were questioned.

My presence among the well-known agitators was mostly accepted, but not always. I just figured that all humans make assumptions about the values and motives of others, and I had to focus on what I could contribute. I didn't try to change to fit in though. I've always believed it takes many different approaches to change the world.

In 1992 the Rights Now group/campaign was born: an umbrella body of large and small, 'of' and 'for' organizations including trade unions. The campaign had strong links with parliamentarians through the All-Party Parliamentary Group for Disability and researcher Victoria Scott. Adam Thomas was the coordinator. They were the pragmatic ambitious glue that kept organizations focused.

Sometimes I could get stuck in too and have a cameo role in the lives of other individuals who were not afraid to lead change via direct action.

The activist group Direct Action Network (DAN), with Barbara Lisicki and Alan Holdsworth as well as people like Liz Carr (who later became an actor and starred in the

UK television series *Silent Witness*), often lead the charge, organizing protests all over London. Disabled individuals would chain themselves to public transport, or to railings outside Parliament, or literally put their bodies on the line by lying down in the roads to stop the traffic. Until then, disabled people were invariably presented as passive recipients of charity. Now, we saw images in the press and on TV of the police gingerly manhandling people without limbs, or in wheelchairs, who were being very feisty and vocal.

Each event was incredibly well organized. Even so, I admit that I was a little nervous in the run-up to my first demonstration, which was to be outside the House of Commons to blockade the MPs' usual entry point. Direct action did not come naturally to me. My preferred strategy was to move things forward by providing the MPs who were on our side with all the ammunition they needed to make the case for legislation. But there was no doubt in my mind this direct action was a necessary instrument of change. It was important to me to lend my support.

When I arrived to help, we were all handed a detailed list of the policies and protocols laid out by DAN. I was designated an 'observer' in case we needed to record the dialogue between the demonstrator and the police. As well as recording dialogue, in theory, the presence of an observer should make sure that the police adhered to the letter of the law and didn't overreach their remit in dealing with individual demonstrators.

I was quite relieved about just having to observe. Pain makes you protect your body, and I was genuinely scared of being thrown to the ground. In this role, I was there to 'keep an eye' on the police. A different, quiet, though no less valuable one.

Backing the freedom fighters

The protests were exciting. I remember the demo for one of DAN's biggest protests: blockading the ITV studios where a 24-hour telethon fundraiser was being filmed. We were furious about the pitiful portrayal of disabled people on the programme. DAN organized a protest group with the provocative strapline of *Piss On Pity*. More than 1,500 protestors turned up to protest in July 1992 and it wasn't a subdued, or boring, protest either. Far from it. The group had its own PA system and musicians with Alan Holdsworth leading the musical march. The demo at times resembled a carnival more than a protest. Vicky Waddington had called me some days earlier. She needed helium which was going to be used to blow up the colourful balloons that festooned the event. This was, as I discovered, quite a challenge. Those cannisters were like full-sized fire extinguishers! There were not many people who could have manhandled the things into place. In the end, I found a way and left work early saying I had a dentist appointment. I had found a supplier, so in an elaborate (and costly!) journey of taxis across London and my blagging the need for volunteers to lift the large cannisters we arrived safely outside the studio. The demo secured masses of coverage.

The obvious question is, how did my sporadic and low-key activism (when compared to the frontline activists) sit with my day job at Arthritis Care? Their policy and, indeed, much of my job centred around changing things from within. We worked with MPs and ministers to encourage and persuade. I followed what I believed then to be the safest strategy; I didn't tell my boss about it. I reasoned that if the worst happened and I was arrested and held overnight, I would deal with the repercussions then. I should add that I did share some of my exploits with some of the MPs that I worked closely with. I remember meeting one at the telethon demo. He was wearing a wig so as not to be recognized. I got a wink. It reminded me of Dad.

The question now though was, would all efforts be enough to bring forth legislation?

A lesson to learn: we must try to recognize our soul in the dark

I have met many thousands of people with disabilities who struggle with very basic 'life requirements' – the day-to-day challenge of getting out of bed (quite literally), getting washed and dressed, getting the kids ready for school, navigating inaccessible services, dealing with inaccessible transport provision, recruitment processes that inappropriately use artificial intelligence (AI) as a screening tool. The list really is endless.

This often 'steals' the time required to focus on our own personal development and the things we can teach ourselves to avoid self-sabotaging aspects of our life.

John Amaechi, in his book *The Promises of Giants*, talks movingly of the moment he shared with his mum, at the age of 16, that he wanted to join the National Basketball

Association.[1] He shares with the readers, quite candidly, that he was a boy who loved pie, curling up with a science-fiction book and daydreaming. So, it was somewhat a shock to his mum to hear her boy talk of his ambition for a wildly incompatible future.

He thinks carefully before explaining his hopes with his mum, and at the end, for good measure, he throws in, 'When I make it, I'll buy you a new house!'

Her response was to ask, 'Would you recognize your soul in the dark?' Then says:

> People who want to do ordinary things are like sticks in the river. They get thrown in at the top, and they may get stuck for a while in some reeds. Or even temporarily washed to the banks. But eventually, all things being equal, they will make their way to the sea. You've chosen an extraordinary destination. And as such, you can't rely on chance or fate to wash you there. People who want to do extraordinary things… they need to be armed with full knowledge of who they are.

She goes on to encourage her son to consider every aspect of who he is and to dig deep. She gets him to think beyond the obvious – beyond age, country of origin, gender identity, etc. She constantly quizzes him: 'What is your most common state or mood? What happens when you experience the extremes of emotion? Under what circumstances do you feel peace, and how often does that occur? What inspires joy and lifts your spirits?'

John has no option but to deal head-on with the inconvenient truth that he was lazy and loved eating pie. He starts a lifelong habit of practising introspection as an integral part of the process of striving to greatness. His mum if she were alive would, I am sure, be proud to see how her son habitually 'recognizes' himself and encourages hundreds of thousands of people to do likewise.

People with disabilities must first deal with the essential and practical aspects of navigating life

I am moved by the knowledge that so many hundreds of thousands of people with disabilities must first deal with the essential and practical aspects of navigating life before being able to view themselves critically, objectively and compassionately. It is hard to look for and recognize your soul in the dark when you are fighting with Social Services for an accessible bathroom. Though if we can, we must.

Practical actions for employers and employees

For employers

USE THE SOCIAL MODEL

The social model of disability has been an important concept in the birth of anti-discrimination legislation and indeed the approach that many employers chose to take when building a disability strategy as part of the overarching diversity and inclusion approach or indeed their sustainable development goals.

If you want to ensure your organization, or indeed any of your own suppliers and customers, takes account of disability in your or their business strategy then take the lead from some of the Valuable 500 organizations that have committed to put disability on their board agendas.

Valuable 500 encourage their tribe of 500 private-sector companies to use the definition of disability set out in the UN Convention on the Rights of Persons with Disabilities (UNCRPD), which aims to set a global standard. The Convention protects all persons with disabilities, who are defined in Article 1 as including:

> those who have long-term physical, mental, intellectual or sensory impairments which in interaction with various barriers may hinder their full and effective participation in society on an equal basis with others.

This is based on the social model and recognizes that disability is an evolving concept, and that people with disabilities are often prevented from exercising their human rights.

Hunt down your own organization's sustainable development goals and statements and check out how far you publicly commit to the process of building long-term improvements for your employees and customers. Ask your own CEO to put disability on the agenda. Make one public commitment. It doesn't matter what sector you work in, ask your CEO to make one public commitment.

LEARN FROM OTHER EMPLOYERS

There are many networks and trade associations that help companies to share best practice and trade information about how to build accessible working worlds as well as products and services. And while there are always commercial sensitivities around the timing of that sharing and networking (and especially when announcing anything new!) it has been, at least to date, a relatively generous space. Make sure your employer is plugged into one or more of the international networks. That might include the International Labour Organization's own Global Business and Disability Network, or Business Disability Forum or the Australian Network on Disability or Disability:IN. In addition to Valuable 500, these employer networks have been, at least to date, the greatest catalysts for employer 'thought-leadership' when it comes to the practical things that can be done to create a level playing field for employees with disability.

While the landscape continues to shift when it comes to the geographical focus of these employer networks, as well as the confusion they sometimes create for employers as to who will provide the greatest 'spark' or source of 'know-how', they remain a vital source of inspiration and ideas for employers. If budget or governance structures precludes your own organization from joining, it is worth accessing the vast library of free resources that they all have produced. Everything you need is out there already. You only need to look.

For employees

BUILD YOUR STORYTELLING SKILLS

Our journeys through life will never be the same. Whether that is because of the age of onset of our disabilities. The severity of onset. The type of disability. Our 'default' personalities. Our access to purposeful and positive advocates in our lives. Our experience of employers' skills at accommodating people with disabilities. Our family experiences. The culture in which we grew up.

Irrespective of the differences in our stories the purple thread that runs through our lives is the complexity of sharing information about our stories with others. Find ways to build your storytelling and information-sharing skills. Seek out the wise counsel of others who have travelled that path. Get yourself a Twitter address or LinkedIn presence. Build in time to connect and watch how others build their brands and identities while remaining authentically aligned to the experience of disability, ill health and neuro divergence.

KEEP LEARNING

They say we teach best what we need to learn. And it is, therefore, no coincidence that in my work I help coach, mentor and teach others about the value of living openly and authentically with the experience of disability.

I have learnt a lot about myself and others by doing so. I still do. The most important thing I have learnt is that it gets better over time. One of my first experiences of sharing my story in the national press was with a women's magazine. I remember spending an exciting lunch with a journalist at Joe Allen's, a trendy restaurant in Central London known for being frequented by journalists. I was horrified when the article was published. She had used words such as 'struck down' with arthritis. That I was 'crippled' with the disease. I wanted the ground to swallow me up. I thought I would never endure the 'pity' of thousands of readers, whom I would never meet. I thought their pity would drown me. It didn't of course. Though I learnt the next time I had a major interview that I would make clear that their description of me would come with some ground rules next time.

So, consider sharing your story. On your terms. Maybe blog or vlog about it. Ask your employer to share your story more widely across the organization. Share the good things. The funny things. The ironic things. Find and share the purpose of your story.

CHAPTER SEVEN

Lonely in a crowd

The FUDs loom large

Fear, uncertainty and doubt. The 'FUDs'. No matter how relentless the demands of the day job I still couldn't quite shake off feelings of loneliness. This is not uncommon for people in my situation. Four times as many people with disability (13 per cent) report feeling lonely 'often or always' compared to those who don't have a disability.[1] One of the big reasons for this is that others don't share your experience. Your life will have taken a turn that you didn't expect and certainly didn't invite. It provokes a deep feeling of sadness and disappointment and an awareness that others won't completely understand because they haven't been through the same thing. People will say, a problem shared is a problem halved. Though many people who experience disability find it hard to share our inner-most thoughts at our lowest points. Why introduce something so dark into other people's lives? Besides, even if you do spill out all your hopes and fears to a trusted companion, it won't change anything. You will still be in the same situation the next day.

Overall, loneliness is born out of fear. No matter what the impairment, whether it is someone who has lost their sight, or is deaf, or experiences mental ill health, those with a disability have a little more to contend with. It might be managing pain, or trips to the hospital, or dealing with less-than-helpful employers or loved ones.

That feeling of incompleteness had been my constant companion ever since my first stay at the Canadian Red Cross Memorial Hospital and had never truly gone away. I was now in a relationship with Peter, whom I had met at the 1992 International Youth Congress, yet there was just a feeling that something was missing. I needed to find my 'red thread' when it came to my 'work calling'.

I suspect that this was why one advert jumped off the page at me when I saw it. There, in among the classifieds in *Disability Now* was an ad that featured words I had never seen together: disabled, leadership and high-performing.

The advert had been placed by what was then known as the Employers' Forum on Disability, now known as Business Disability Forum (BDF). It had been founded by Susan Scott-Parker in 1991 as the first business disability network working for the mutual benefit of businesses and disabled people. One of her first (of many) moves was to create a Disability Standard to measure and benchmark corporate disability performance. The idea behind it was to create the *business* case for

The idea was to create the business case for talent, rather than the moral or charitable one

talent, rather than simply thinking about the moral or charitable one. This was a hugely valuable and long over-due exercise, which was also an important steppingstone on the way to realizing the big goal: anti-discrimination legislation.

Central to the BDF's strategy was working with vanguard organizations that were prepared to take risks. On the side she had also teamed up with the high-end leadership and management consultancy Coverdale and created the world's first leadership development programme for people with a disability. The ad I was look-ing at was offering a bursary for the first intake on this programme. There were three bursaries on offer and, as I read the criteria, all I could think was: I want this!

Meeting fellow travellers

As well as my CV and details of my work history, the application process also required applicants to list their 10 greatest achievements. This was tough. What were the 10 greatest achievements of Brand Kate?

Perhaps the word brand is rather grandiose, but the idea of building a brand around us is a helpful concept, whatever our ambitions. We all need an understanding of what we bring to the world. Do we get things done? Are we a collaborator? Do we make others feel good in a room? Do we shoulder the tasks that no one else wants to do? Once you know who you are, you can feel good about your contribution and that is a crucial part of confidence in the workplace.

I spent a long time writing and then rewriting my supposed life triumphs. I wanted to sound interesting and well-rounded. After many false starts, I went for a mix of personal and professional achievements. I wrote about the challenges of getting into university and achieving two degrees, but also about how I had found a fantastic group of amazing friends while doing so. There was the difficult time I had learnt how to walk again after surgery, but then the pride at being an active part of the political process that was working towards the law that would improve things for every person with a disability in the workplace. I must have done something right as I was invited in for an interview.

I was a nervous wreck before the interview which was happening in what was then the plush HQ of Midland Bank (later HSBC), and the sight of the grand entrance did nothing to calm my nerves. Fifteen minutes before my interview, I managed to force myself to walk through the doors of the bank HQ, stepping nervously onto the fantastic Lutyens-designed, art deco reception area, with its striking black-and-white checkered floor. I felt in a complete daze. What was I doing there? I was used to the threadbare carpets of the voluntary sector.

As I stepped out of the lift Susan Scott-Parker stepped forward to greet me. She seemed to know exactly who I was and immediately took complete command of the conversation. She was flamboyant and utterly mesmerizing. Interestingly though, for someone who clearly had such a strong personality, the conversation was not all about her. Susan didn't just know exactly who I was, she'd clearly read my application very closely. Within a matter of moments, she was picking out key events from my achievements list and pressing me for more details. This may sound like the beginning of a terrible ordeal, but her approach put me completely at ease. It was great to add a little more detail to my own, personal brand.

After my brief meeting with Susan, and following the panel interview, I wanted that bursary more than ever and I was completely over the moon when a few days later, I was told that I had won a place on the scheme. The other two successful candidates were also very active in the disability movement. Susan was looking for people who could use the training to good effect.

The power of great mentors

In taking up the Coverdale Leadership Development Bursary scheme I now had access to leadership training from some of the UK's top firms including Midland and Barclays banks, the Post Office and Coverdale. We were offered access to their usual leadership programmes for their own management fast-track, completely free of charge. Each month I attended a course of a couple of days or sometimes a full week, given by the most incredibly clever, experienced and knowledgeable people. The thought leaders who ran these courses wanted us to discover and then develop our innate leadership style.

We each had a dedicated professional mentor and mine was one of the senior consultants at Coverdale. He helped me start to think in a new way.

In my career to date, I had already been fortunate enough to meet and learn from several amazing mentors and my Coverdale mentor was equally helpful, setting a pattern of mentorship that would continue throughout my career. Mentors are a hugely important part of career development, and I would always recommend to everyone to seek one, or preferably several, out. They help you think about your place in the working world. Seeking and accepting feedback is not always easy, but it shows you what you need to learn, or skills you need to develop. It can be challenging, but you'd be foolish to ignore these nuggets of advice.

People are usually flattered to be asked to act as mentors. If they can't do it for any reason, which is normally to do with not enough time, they will often recommend someone else. You can help your own prospects by 'packaging' your mentorship. In other words, demonstrate that there is a beginning, middle and end. 'Can I have one hour of your time each week for six weeks? The timing can be of your choosing. This is the problem I am trying to address… .' If you ask, it is rare to be turned down. The point here is, it is well worth seeking out mentors because they will help you substantially improve your performance.

What I learnt most from that incredible bursary is that everything is possible and that it is OK to be more masterful about our destinies than we sometimes chose to believe. To be who you want to be, you need to be authentic. You need to own who you are, warts and all. I also learnt that it is far more effective to be your own biggest critic. Yes, you need to invite criticism, even if that criticism seems tough, or even a little unpalatable, or seemingly unbearable. But you have to examine your own behaviour first and foremost.

Making the most of the legislation

Towards the end of 1993 I had come to the end of my leadership bursary, so my day-to-day contact with Susan was due to end. By this stage, Susan Scott-Parker was helping employers to understand the business case for anti-discrimination legislation as well as encouraging them to sponsor the enabling tools to drive internal change. While many businesses were starting to step up, there seemed a lot more to do both with the bursaries and with the other BDF projects elsewhere. Susan had much to do, and only two part-time staff. She asked if I wanted a paid-for secondment to help her recruit members. By this stage, Richard Gutch had taken over from Jean Gaffin at Arthritis Care. Fortunately, he agreed to let me go on secondment from Arthritis Care to help build the BDF membership and recruit the next 100 employers.

It couldn't have been a more exciting time to be involved in the BDF full time. We were, by now, in the final months and weeks of the hard-fought battle to get into law what would become the Disability Discrimination Act 1995. There were, as there always are, some compromises to be made along the way and a whole lot of last-minute negotiations. The biggest sticking point was the same one as it had been throughout the entire process: the notion of 'reasonable adjustment', which defined the policy that firms had to follow when providing access to goods, facilities, services and premises. Hours and hours of time were spent debating the true meaning of those two, usually most innocuous, words. Was 'reasonableness' the cop-out that employers would use to say any changes were just too arduous and disruptive? That was certainly what the hard-liners thought. On the other side were those who were looking at it from the employers' point of view and who were nervous about doing anything that might disrupt businesses too much. Multiple questions were asked about who could decide what was reasonable or not: the employer, the employee or just the courts? For a long time, it felt like the argument would never be resolved, but finally it was and the idea of 'reasonable adjustment' became enshrined in law on 2 December 1994.

While there will always be detractors who say the new law did not go far enough, it was a victory. The concept of adjustment was law in the UK. Plus, most crucially, it would make it illegal for employers to say at interview: sorry, you can't do this job at all.

Changing tack

If you look at any people movement, whether Black civil rights, or women's liberation, or LGBT+ rights, the battle doesn't end once legislation has been changed. That's just the beginning. Everyone has a part to play in making sure things improve. BDF now had more of a role than ever in finding a way to support employers and offering the enabling products to build inclusive workplaces. There were a lot of organizations that felt very nervous about it and didn't properly understand what it meant and what their policies should now look like. BDF was in the perfect position to help.

I didn't want to simply help employers to understand the new legislation and embed the disability-specific equalities into their day-to-day strategies though. The goal had to be for them to fully embrace it. In other words, I wanted to help them become disability-confident organizations, rather than ones doing the bare minimum to comply and keep themselves out of trouble.

I wanted to help them become disability-confident organizations

A big part of that confidence was awakening organizations to the amazing pool of talent that they had access to. Susan had conceived of the term 'disability confident' while at BDF and it was a powerful instrument of change. The employers' community was starting to get into its stride though I still didn't quite know where I needed to go next and what I needed to do to 'mine' the new mood music.

My time at BDF was exciting but I felt I needed to spread my wings and asked if I could take on the leadership bursary scheme. By this stage, I had quite a few ideas on how I could expand it, bring in more sponsors and get more funding. I couldn't continue to do so on secondment from Arthritis Care, so I handed in my notice so I could go it alone. I set up The Leadership Consortium in December 1995, with some initial funding from Northern Rock building society. I set about organizing a programme that emulated the one we'd all originally been through. The mission was very similar: set up high-end leadership bursaries for some talented people that might otherwise be overlooked. Susan gave it her 'blessing' as well as agreeing to be on the advisory board and let me have a desk at BDF offices to run the new scheme.

How to start a storytelling movement

In the first year The Leadership Consortium offered 15 bursaries. We already had powerful supporters. We benefited hugely from the involvement of the civil service, via Lord Robin Butler, who was a big advocate for the scheme. In fact, Robin wanted the civil services' disabled fast-trackers scheme to benefit from our bursary programme and learn from it. What I liked about his involvement was that he was prepared to be a visible senior ally and wanted to enable disabled talent in the civil service to flourish.

As well as signing up sponsors I also needed to convince them to offer places on their management training schemes. After that, I had to work closely with each one to find mentors and then match them up with the people to whom we'd awarded bursaries. What surprised even me was the calibre of people who came forward to offer their time as mentors. Many were in top-tier management positions and, as more people came on board, it became self-perpetuating, since there was a real kudos to becoming involved with The Leadership Consortium scheme among such esteemed company. The involvement of all these big names made our scheme even more sought after by potential bursaries too. Winning a place became a prestigious event.

The sponsors were not just offering places on their internal management training schemes either. Each one was asked to put forward cash to help fund the scheme. Most donated £15,000, but if ever I saw the chance to ask for more, I went for it. I remember receiving a gentle kick under the table from the CEO of Coverdale when we were on a visit to the Royal Mail, when I doubled 'the ask' to £30,000.

The experience of dealing with big corporates and very senior executives was completely different to what I had been doing at Arthritis Care. Initially, it was terrifying. Every time I stepped into a high-roofed atrium of a blue-chip organization, ready to ask for as much time, sponsorship and support as they could spare, I had to fight back emotions that I was not the right person to do this. I was not good enough. The classic imposter phenomenon. In their 1978 study Clance and Imes study first started to use the term.[2] For them, it was experienced by high-achieving women who believe they are not bright and have fooled anyone who thinks otherwise.

This feeling of not being worthy dogs so many people of difference

I knew only too well that this feeling of not being worthy dogs so many people of difference. A lifetime of experiencing negative attitudes can take its toll. Even though my doubts were totally unfounded because I did know exactly what I was doing, it didn't help quell the nerves.

This was the period when I began to recognize the power of storytelling. In the early days I found it quite hard to find the right tone of voice. I couldn't simply breeze in and tell everyone what they needed to do. Likewise, I was not keen on the 'help us now, because it might be you with a disability in the future' style of argument. Yes, it was possible to back this up with some great statistics about how incidents of disability rise with age, but that doesn't really seem like a very positive or compelling message. I decided that a different approach was best. Everybody knows somebody with a disability. Perhaps a friend, or someone in the family has a health condition. When I began to relate the stories of some of the hundreds of people I had met over the years there always seemed to be something that most others could relate to. They knew individuals who have struggled in a variety of ways, whether it is getting access to basic amenities, or finding a job, or finding the support to achieve their full potential when they were in work. Through making the link with that personal connection, others will understand that it can be hard for employees with disabilities to navigate their way.

Fortunately, thanks to the Disability Discrimination Act 1995, as well as the groundwork laid within the business community, I was, in some ways pushing at an open door. Business leaders were beginning to recognize that disability was a business issue and about making sure organizations had access to the absolute best pool of talent. While I say some organizations were more receptive, it was not always easy though. There were still many entrenched views, and some people took a lot of persuading that it was in their interests or possible.

'We'd have to make too many adjustments,' they'd say.

Or 'We need people to answer the phone, how will that work with someone who can't hear?'

I would patiently describe that there are ways and means and multiple accessible tools to enable an accessible playing field. I'd use examples of real-life people, making a huge impact once they'd been given the ways and means. Organizations just needed to be willing to try. And, meanwhile, back to the talent message.

I did mini self-reviews after each meeting I held. *I went in too hard.* Or, *that was too little.* Or, *that went a bit wrong!* And, very occasionally, *that was pitch perfect!* I constantly reviewed my performance and was often hard on myself. Some individuals were exceptionally generous too. On one occasion, I did a speech at Midland Bank which, after my usual self-review, I concluded had gone OK. Not brilliant, but OK. Afterwards, as I mingled with everyone during the reception, I was approached by Peter Hobbs. Peter's CV was a who's who of directorships of top organizations, from the Wellcome Trust foundation to Contemporary Applied Arts to the Chemical Industries Association, so I felt quite pleased when he told me that I'd made a 'fantastic' speech. Though I think he was being kind in order to warm up to an offer which was to fund me to work with McAlinden Associates, an organization that trains politicians and business leaders to speak more persuasively.

After a short while he returned with a confirmation. Diageo, one of McAlinden's clients, had agreed to open a place for me on one of their training courses. It was an amazing opportunity. Public speaking was something I needed to nail. I know most people find it daunting, but it wasn't that. I didn't mind getting up in front of a big group of people; I just didn't feel I was doing it particularly well, which may have meant I wasn't getting the message across.

The two-day course was a revelation. I was the only woman there, among six other senior male Diageo executives. Part of the training process included us speaking in front of each other from a speech we had made in the past. We would then give each other feedback about what we did and didn't do well. They talked about Tia Maria and sales figures and wore black suits. I talked about disability rights and wore a frock. It was as excruciating as it sounds doing something like this in front of complete strangers. They immediately homed in on my body language regarding my talk, in particular the use of my hands. Ever since my teens, I had been self-conscious about them. My go-to-solution had been to fold my arms or put my hands behind my back. My fellow course members explained that this made me stand awkwardly and stiffly which just made me look nervous and subsequently detracted from the message.

It's hard to describe how painful it was to have that direct conversation about my hands in front of this group of men. I'd never met them before and it could so easily have felt horribly exposing. Yet, they were wonderful.

'Be who you are,' was the advice they all gave. 'If you want to make a point, use your hands to emphasize that point. Wear more of your rings. If people are going to look, give them something sparkling to remember you by.'

My abiding memory of that course was laughing, a lot, with kind individuals who were not shy in offering difficult feedback in a way that was useful. I came out of it understanding more techniques to use in my quest to become an authentic and powerful speaker. When I had packed my bag and was heading to my car for the drive home I spotted a bottle of liqueur on the roof of the car, waiting for me. It was just a kind, 'see ya around' gift from one of the Diageo sales executives. I received it as a 'go girl' from one of the globe's largest brands that had helped me over a few demons about how to tell their story in an authentic way. I got a lifelong taste for Tia Maria for all the right reasons.

A lesson to learn: people cannot second guess you

For all the challenges in securing work, I have always lived on the assumption that the world does not owe me a living and organizations are full of people trying to get by. I could never 'assume' an employer would immediately see the potential I could offer. They had to get past some pretty raw truths. My stamina was impaired. My ability to walk was impaired. I could not lift boxes or do piles of photo-copying or all the thousands of mundane things you often needed to do as a junior member of staff. Sometimes you don't get what you need because it doesn't occur to others, or indeed yourself, to do things a bit differently.

I was reminded of this when reading *Lean In* by Sheryl Sandberg.[3] She writes of her time when pregnant with her first child in the summer of 2004. She spends a rough morning staring at the bottom of the toilet and then rushing to get to an important client meeting. At the time she is working for Google and the company was growing so fast that parking was a problem and the only spot she could find was far away. She rushes to her meeting though it makes her nausea worse, and she worries whether she can get through her sales pitch.

Says Sandberg:

> That night, I recounted these troubles to my husband Dave. He pointed out that Yahoo, where he worked at the time, had designated parking for expectant mothers at the front of each building. The next day, I marched in – or more like waddled in – to see Google founders Larry Page and Sergey Brin in their office... I found Sergey in a yoga position in the corner and announced that we needed pregnancy parking, preferably sooner rather than later. He looked up at me and agreed immediately, noting that he had never thought about it before.

Sandberg reflects on how she felt embarrassed that she had not realized that pregnant women needed reserved parking until she experienced her own aching feet.

This is true with many things in life.

Practical actions for employers and employees

For employers

USE STRENGTHS-BASED RECRUITMENT

Consider using a strengths-based approach to recruitment such as the way EY does for graduate and other recruitment. I have experienced strengths-based applications several times in my career and it is a great way for employers to discover the core skills of individuals. EY is a successful advocate of the method and routinely refer to its value in helping people with disabilities dig a little deeper in describing the skills and strengths they have by managing disability, ill health or neuro-divergence.[4]

REMEMBER THE DISABILITY CONFIDENCE CONCEPTS

Remind yourself of the four key concepts that made up the original concept 'Disability Confidence'.[5] These include the requirement for employers to:

- understand that disability impacts all parts of the business
- identify and remove barriers for groups of people
- be willing and able to adjust things for individuals
- not make assumptions based on peoples' disability

They remain the bedrock of all successful change programmes.

For employees

DISPEL THE IMPOSTER SYNDROME

While many will experience the imposter phenomenon in our lives, we do truly have to find a way to manage it.

Colin Diedrich writes in 2018:

> I'm a scientist with a learning disability. I've also struggled with imposter syndrome my entire life. To me imposter syndrome is the feeling that I don't belong or deserve my success, and that everyone around me will think I'm a fraud. Having learning disabilities has made coping with imposter syndrome not just a challenge for me – but a battle.

He goes on:

> I thought when I received my college degree I'd no longer
> feel like an imposter. I was wrong. Then I thought when I got
> my PhD in molecular virology and microbiology, I'd leave
> imposter syndrome behind. I didn't. I was convinced that
> the closer I got to my dream of becoming a scientist, the
> more I'd feel at home with my success. But that's not what
> happened.[6]

Manage your imposter.

ALWAYS SHARE YOUR STRENGTHS

Whether asked to or not, create the lifelong habit of
sharing your strengths at interview or at promotion.
Everyone has a different way of doing this. Some of us will
prefer a straightforward approach and will weave in a
reference to our disability at the same time as displaying
our competencies. Others may prefer to use a 'humble-
brag' about our skills and strengths: a seemingly modest or
self-deprecating statement about our lived experience of
disability with the actual intention of drawing attention to
something of which we are proud. Whatever you do, cultivate the skill of sharing your strengths born from the
challenge of navigating inaccessible environments or
inappropriate reactions to our lives.

CHAPTER EIGHT

Eradicating shame

Creating parties with purpose

In 2001, a full six years after the Disability Discrimination Act (DDA), a lot of employers were still floundering when it came to good practice. It wasn't that they weren't willing to comply, because the majority were (some because they had to), but many organizations still needed a lot of advice and support about how to adapt policies, practices and procedures in practical terms. What does a workplace adjustment mean for someone who has dyslexia, or a hearing impairment? How do organizations deal with someone with a mental health condition who occasionally has bleak days and just doesn't want to talk?

I was still an associate of BDF, which I had been since the bursary. It was an unpaid honorary role and had continued to be a consistent part of my life. It constantly brought me into contact with a lot of people whom I had known for years, in one capacity or another, including the indefatigable Susan Scott-Parker. We often shared the same platform at speaking gigs. Plus, of course, Susan was constantly roping me in on other activities.

'I've got a round table, being hosted by Sainsbury's and the CEO will be there,' she'd announce. 'You should be there.'

Or 'The CEO of McDonald's is hosting such and such MP for a lunch and I've managed to nobble a couple of places. Can you be at the Dorchester tomorrow?'

I never said no. This was the best training in perfecting the art of persuasion that I had been working on for years. How do you get people to change their minds? You stay real, outline the problem and offer engaging solutions. Parties with a purpose. We had a well-worn and hugely effective routine too, based on Susan's mantra that in order to talk the hard stuff, you need to talk the small stuff first. Thus, Susan and I would wait until the executives had a few glasses of wine under their belt and chatted about this or that, then Susan would turn to me, natural as you like, and say: Kate, tell them that story about your interview when you were asked about what you could not do.

Asking better questions

This would be my cue to tell a story about 'that moment' or indeed any one of the hundreds of injustices that I had experienced or heard about. The stories weren't told in a hectoring or negative way. I was careful to inject just the right amount of humour. The important thing was to get the message across and give influential people something to mull over. Something to do. I wanted them to consider how individuals moved themselves through medical diagnosis and the subsequent period of adjustment at the same time as doing the day job. How did they feel about sharing information about their health or disability? How did they build individual resilience? It all built a picture of how the experience of difference could add value to people's skills and competencies. These individuals could and indeed should be role models and catalysts for change within their own organizations. Then, when we came knocking on the door of our lunch companions in the future, asking them to consider sponsoring a new bursary, or launching a new mentorship programme, they would be more receptive to it. That is how change happens.

I'd been learning my trade all the time. I'd lived through the days of activism, where hundreds of people took direct action to ensure the right changes were made. Now we were in the midst of a time where a different approach was required to see those changes properly implemented. Behavioural change will always start with a 'have to': the legislation. It is what pushes people to change. But to make it happen

Behavioural change will always start with a 'have-to': the legislation

properly, you need to take people with you. That takes time. And of course I wasn't the only one learning this new trade. Some of the other BDF associates were sublime at their trade and I was learning so much from them. I worked with so many remarkable people.

What is this term 'reasonable'?

What concerned me most in the aftermath of the legislation was how the concept of 'reasonable adjustment' had started to be hijacked. I had never had a big problem with the idea when it was added to the Bill. However, over time, there seemed to be a growing movement to 'interpret' it, most of which was going in completely the wrong direction as far as I could tell. Businesses would publish policies on 'reasonable adjustment processes', or appoint a 'reasonable adjustment coordinator'. After a while, it seemed to be getting out of hand. I couldn't help but think: no business in its right mind would talk about its reasonable maternity leave policy, or its reasonable flexible working policy, or reasonable annual leave allowance. In other words, we take it for granted that any adjustments made will be entirely reasonable. Why then, were employers prefacing everything to do with disability with the adjective 'reasonable'? By doing this, all anyone could focus on was reasonable, rather than the more important verb 'adjustment'. It is, after all, the adjustment that matters. When you focus on 'reasonable', the conversation begins from entirely the wrong place and will inevitably go off track from there. Yes, you could say businesses were doing their best to understand and interpret the legislation, but such rigid thinking destroyed all creativity. It also completely eroded what we were trying to do in showing that people of difference are a talented bunch that need to be onboard, not a drain on resources.

My suspicion is that the lack of imagination when it came to adjustments was in part down to the haste with which HR and diversity professionals scrambled to get moving on policies that complied with the new law back in 1995. It was a useful shorthand to brand the concept internally, but over time, the wording was blocking any flair in the interpretation. Perhaps too, the wording masked something that no one really wanted to articulate: that any adjustments needed to be made at a reasonable *cost*.

There was something else that bothered me too: why was it that there was not more challenge from employees with disability, when it came to the overuse of 'reasonable' when linked with adjustment/accommodation? Did that, in some way, mean that individuals in this situation were somehow not convinced of their own worth? The widespread tendency to concede to employers' needs to make adjustments both affordable and practicable seemed to indicate this. I wondered if we were reaching a point where we needed to switch the focus a little, from employer to employee. While we needed to press the point about disability-confident employers, we needed employees with disability to be part of the conversation too. As employees with disability, we had to recognize that we had skin in the game; that it was time we identified the things necessary for us to get ahead at work, to share our own experiences about how to build personal resilience and how to be ourselves at work for our personal and business benefit.

It seemed to me that there was a lot more work for me to do and, perhaps, I would be better suited to do something that tackled the next strategic challenges of the day – maybe build a new employee 'movement'? And then I saw the advert for the job of chief executive of RADAR (now Disability Rights UK). How could I resist? This was one of the central organizations that, with others, had secured the DDA.

A lesson to learn: employers cannot compensate for a person's past, but they can offer a new future

As described by the United Nations, employment data on persons with disabilities is hard to come by.[1] Though of the data that does exist the picture suggests that around the globe the same facts hold true. There are more people with disabilities than most people assume and the employment gap between people with disabilities and non-disabled people is significant.

In the UK, for example, 20 per cent of the working-age population report having a disability and 33 per cent of the working-age population report having a long-term health condition.[2]

In the UK 20 per cent of the working-age population report having a disability

In 2021 the disability employment rate in the UK was 52.7 per cent compared to 81 per cent for non-disabled people. And while 380,000 workless disabled people move into work on average each year, around 340,000 disabled workers move out of work.[3]

In the United States in 2021, 19.1 per cent of persons with a disability were employed compared with 63.7 per cent for persons without a disability.[4]

In India, only 36 per cent of India's 26 million people with disabilities are employed.[5]

At first glance these statistics may feel 'odd.' That is because definitions of disability vary across the world and even where they are robust within a certain country, and 'generously' include people who are defined by disability according to the impact of their experience on day-to-day living (as opposed to a percentage bodily deficit) it is notoriously hard to secure accurate data because of fear of stigma. It is often hard too for people who first experience disability to know that they may be protected by legislation. We simply don't pick up the knowledge in our former privileged non-disabled lives and identities.

What is clear is that the individual personal challenge of navigating the early days of ill health and disability can have as much, and sometimes more, of an impact on being able to secure work, than any physical or cultural or legislative barriers that may exist.

Employers cannot compensate for a person's past, but by adopting good practice in recruitment, adjustment processes, disability leave management, supply chain management, product advertising and connecting their diversity strategy with the UN's sustainable development goals they can be part of the process of creating new futures.

And of all the practical things an employer can do, far and away the easiest is to build the duty to make a workplace adjustment/accommodation and determine standard service level agreements by which they are delivered into their DNA. Creating an elegant, seamless workplace adjustment/accommodation process for either those who may acquire a disability for the first time at work or for those people with disabilities who start as new employees is one of the most powerful actions. Though you would be surprised by how many organizations make the disability inclusion piece more complex than it needs to be by simply avoiding the fact that the process is likely to need re-engineering. It can take effort, systems thinkers and table thumpers to create a system with clear accountabilities as well as service level agreements. They are often a mess with responsibilities split between many people and departments.

There are various theories why this is so. One is that organizations assume the costs of adjustments are more than they actually are, so lead persons feel they are opening a hornet's nest if they start to surface the need to improve the process. Another is that organizations believe the number of people with disability they employ is low, so why bother improving a process that is rarely used? Others will suggest that employers will fear that by streamlining the service you make it easier for people who are not 'entitled' to adjust-

Organizations assume the costs of adjustments are more than they actually are

ments to apply for and secure them. We call that 'chair-envy' at PurpleSpace. The envy of privileged non-disabled people who would like 'fancier kit' trumping (and over-taking) the needs of colleagues with legitimate need for 'kit' because it simply gets them to first base.

Of course, all these things play a part to a lesser or greater extent, but my career has taught me two other things along the way. The first is that because the experience of disability and ill health is often a story of transition (from one identity to another) that can take many years to make sense of, the 'needs' we may have at work are eclipsed by some of the more basic and domestic needs we have. Add to that, we often try to 'protect' others from our sadness, our discomfort, our fear because to say these things out loud will often cause internal distress and I know very few employees with disabilities who enjoy getting distressed at work. This has meant an 'under-developed' community of out, loud and proud employees with disabilities insisting that their employers get their act together in the same way that women did when maternity provision became the norm.

In terms of the average costs of workplace adjustments, it is hard to access accurate figures though there is some emerging evidence that the costs are negligible, especially when compared with the other types of adjustment costs that employers make, such as maternity provision. A poll commissioned by executive search firm Inclusive Boards suggests the average cost of an adjustment is about £75 per person.[6] Business Disability Forum suggests the average cost of making an adjustment is less than £180.[7]

A study well worth reading comes from the work of Lloyds Banking Group (LBG) between 2012 and 2014. They re-engineered and invested in their then ad hoc 'reasonable adjustment process' to create a carefully designed 'workplace adjustment service', emphasizing a change of ethos to supporting employees to meet their needs and to optimizing their contribution at work rather than compliance with legislation. They deliberately re-branded the process the 'workplace adjustment process' rather than use the more common term 'reasonable adjust-ment' process, to reinforce the message that they were working towards the mutual benefit of individuals and the bank, and not grounding the process in legal compliance.

This substantively different approach included:

- appointing a business manager as a process owner (not HR or Occupational Health) to be responsible for the speed, efficiency and continual improvement of the end-to-end process
- centralizing funding rather than using line managers' local budgets to pay for adjustments and making costs anonymous so they cannot be traced back to the individual colleague, thus removing any localized disincentives to pay for adjustments
- empowering colleagues to self-refer into a centralized process, this removing the reliance on their line manager to initiate the adjustment process
- establishing a single, well-publicized point of entry staffed by experienced people and geared to provide adjustments as 'straight through orders' when possible, thus eliminating unnecessary assessments
- creating a catalogue of pre-approved IT and other physical adjustments
- creating a policy on non-physical adjustments to improve colleague, manager and assessor understanding in non-physical adjustments and to speed up decision making
- ensuring effective management accountability for the speed and effectiveness of the entire end-to-end process

In a detailed study about the experience of LBG conducted by Business Disability Forum and Microlink, researchers saw that during the years 2012 to 2014 approximately 18,893 colleagues used the service from a total population of just under 100,000 (approximately 19 per cent of the workforce).[8] Key benefits from the investment included:

- The average assessment and service cost per case decreased from £750 in 2010 to £500 in March 2014, a decrease of 34 per cent.
- The numbers needing formal assessments dropped from 80 per cent to 43 per cent in the first three months, generating cost savings of more than £125,000 for LBG.
- 62 per cent of colleagues (and 63 per cent of their managers) using the service reported a reduction in absence levels. To illustrate, every single day where sickness absence is reduced among the cohort that benefited from the workplace adjustment service equates to a productivity gain of £1.193 million. This was modelled based on 62 per cent of the 18,893 people that engaged with the service reducing absence by just one day each and where each staff member's average weekly earnings is £26,500.

This study has been a much under-reported story of the energy and appetite of one company to understand what they can do to help their people access workplace adjustments as easily and quickly as possible.

Practical actions for employers and employees

For employers

INVESTIGATE THE PERCEPTION GAP

Get some baseline information about the perceptions that employees may have of employers. In a study by Accenture in 2020 entitled 'Getting to Equal: Disability inclusion' they unpacked the eight factors that unlock inclusivity. It draws on a global survey of companies across industries of almost 6,000 employees with disabilities, 1,748 executives (of whom 675 have disabilities) and 50 video interviews.

The study highlighted a perception gap between what leaders think is happening and what employees with disabilities think is the reality – a disconnect that underscores a lack of openness on both sides. The researchers calculated the impact of improving workplace culture on the confidence and engagement levels of persons with disabilities and on companies' potential for growth:

> When employees with disabilities feel less sure that
> their talents are being utilized, they are less likely to
> thrive. If bosses aren't speaking out about inclusion, if
> accommodations aren't being made, and if employees don't
> feel they can raise concerns about how they're treated, then
> secrecy reigns and both employees and organizations can't
> reach their potential.

SUPPORT LEADERS WITH DISABILITY

Notice the need to support your C-suite leaders from sharing their experiences of disability. In 2019 Ernst & Young conducted some research entitled 'Disability Confidence: The business leadership imperative'. They found that business leaders with disabilities are twice as likely to be underrepresented in companies globally: though one in seven of the world's population live with a disability, fewer than half this figure (1 in 14, or 7 per cent) of board-level executives consider themselves to have a disability.

Of these, one in five do not feel comfortable 'admitting' their disability to colleagues – highlighting the fact that disability continues to be a taboo subject for many of the world's leading businesses. It is likely that it gets harder to identify with the experience of disability the closer you get to C-suite level.

For employees

SAY YES TO EVERYTHING

If you want to be one of the future out, loud and proud disabled C-suite leaders, say yes to everything. There is an inspiring TED talk from 2016 by Shonda Rhimes about how she said yes to everything over the course of a year, in which she says 'The very act of doing the thing that scared me undid the fear.' She talks about how the word 'yes' changed her life.[9]

We often hear 'no'. No, we cannot get adequate housing stock. No, we cannot meet your basic healthcare needs. No, we can't offer you an immediate workplace adjustment/accommodation. No can sometimes swamp our existence.

It means we sometimes must work harder to generate the 'yeses' – even if we have to do that ourselves.

BEWARE THE VELVET RAGE

In 2005 Alan Downs published a remarkable book about overcoming the pain of growing up gay in a straight man's world. It is a powerful reminder of the struggle we often have amidst the barrage of daily reminders that we are not the norm.[10] The 'lack of reinforcement of who you are takes a deep emotional toll. This anger pushes me at times to overcompensate and try to earn love and acceptance by being more, better, beautiful.' It is a powerful book to remind ourselves to notice the purple velvet rage and the emotional challenge of self-discovery, irrespective of external barriers. We need to find the contentment in being us.

CHAPTER NINE

Ensuring an organization is better for having you there

Reinventing the instruments of change

Getting the job as chief executive of RADAR was a big deal and I was determined to make my mark. I was, however, under no delusions about how tough the task ahead was going to be. My number one priority was to mobilize our membership to make manifest the Disability

Just because the law had been passed didn't mean every employer was adhering to it

Discrimination Act (DDA) legislation. It would have been too easy to sit back and say 'we've done it' (particularly since it had been in place for more than half a decade) but we hadn't. As I already knew all too well, just because the law had been passed didn't mean every employer was properly adhering to it. We had to continue to beat the drum about the issues that had made the legislation necessary in the first place.

When I joined RADAR, I was determined not to be held back by the *fear* of making mistakes (and being judged on them). I was certainly prepared to put my neck on the line and to be quite vocal about my thoughts on how the world can and should change. It was hard to escape the sheer weight of responsibility though. It was my first chief executive role and the idea took a little getting used to.

As I accepted the position, I couldn't help thinking about the achievements of other, similar movements which had a quarter of a century head-start on us and were still battling hard to meet their goals. In the UK the Sex Discrimination Act 1975 had been in place for a quarter of a century by now and yet reports of gender inequality appeared with depressing regularity. Everywhere you looked there were stories about extreme pay gaps, or about lack of female representation at senior levels in every profession. The same went for the Racial Discrimination Act that had been passed in the same year. Things had changed, yes, but progress was achingly slow and it was obvious there was so much still to do.

What, I wondered, could I learn from the Equal Opportunities Commission and the Commission for Racial Equality which had been set up in the aftermath of both Acts? Perhaps they had some pointers that might help me move things along. In preparation for taking up my appointment, I went to see their respective chairs, Dame Julie Mellor and Baron Herman Ouseley. My question to them both was simple: here we were, 25 years on, what would be their biggest piece of advice to someone in my position? The response from the pair was the same: 'Don't take your foot off the gas pedal. Not ever. The job is not done. The job is never done.'

Improving legislation

I had a very long 'to-do' list. While the DDA had taken us a big step forward, there were still large gaps in the legislation. There were several changes that urgently needed to be made in the transport and built environment, for example. Building regulations allowed for numerous exemptions from the legislation and in other areas there were what felt like gargantuan lead-in times before any meaningful changes came into effect. Take rolling stock and train carriages as a case in point. Upgrades were only mandatory once units had outlived their working lives and needed to be upgraded. That eventuality could be as much as 25 years away for some of the newer models.

There was also still work to be done to ensure the parts of the legislation that could be implemented straight away were properly understood. On the employer's side, the onus was on employees to say that they have a disability, whereupon the employer will then endeavour to make the required reasonable adjustment/accommodation. Employers could, therefore, sit tight until one of their team raised an issue and if employees were reluctant to do so, or didn't know their rights, the entire system would break down. To be fair to employers, any lack of adherence to the rules was not always wilful: many simply didn't understand exactly what they were required to do. Despite the burgeoning industry advising on reasonable adjustments/accommodation, what did it mean, for example, to make a 'reasonable adjustment/accommodation' for someone with a mental health condition? There was a pressing need for an ongoing education process to make the new rules clear in as broad a way as possible.

Another part of the legislation that had received less publicity for some reason was the bit that focused on how organizations served goods and services to the public. The requirement here was for what is known as an 'anticipatory duty'. Thus, a large supermarket would have to anticipate that a significant proportion of its customers would have a disability and make the necessary adjustments to allow them to access all parts of the store safely and comfortably. There was a huge range of work that needed to be done here to support businesses providing goods and services and to make sure the relevant adjustments were properly enacted.

As if that was not enough, there were still profound inequities in the provision of both primary and secondary healthcare. While education had been ostensibly 'tackled' by the Special Educational Needs and Disabilities Act, which was passed around the same time as the DDA, and was supposed to establish the equivalent rights for children in education, there was a general feeling that with funding tight, young people could be last to the party when it came to meaningful change.

Once the DDA had been passed, one of the big goals was to give people with disability a more distinctive voice in government. The preferred option was a government commission, not unlike the Equal Opportunities Commission, or the Commission for Racial Equality, which would make sure everyone adhered to the legislation. It took five more long years of campaigning before the government finally agreed to

One of the goals was to give people with disability a more distinctive voice in government

set up the Disability Rights Commission (DRC). The obvious choice to chair it was Bert Massie, who had led RADAR through the 1990s and who was widely agreed to have been instrumental in securing the DDA legislation. Thus, this was how the role at the top of RADAR had fallen free.

The creation of DRC after such a long campaign was greeted with much fanfare and, of course, everyone wanted to be part of it. It was not difficult for Bert Massie to poach the really big talent to join him there. He also fished extensively from the RADAR pool and tempted away many of his old colleagues. In a short space of time, he had managed to gather around him all the best in the business. Of course, this left some gaping holes elsewhere, not least at RADAR where nearly all of the senior team had left, as well as most of the people in the tiers below that.

I'd known during the interview stage for the RADAR job that nearly everyone was heading off. It was hard not to. Even so, it was a huge shock when I arrived at RADAR, having got the job. The place was an empty shell. There was little I could do about it though and no point dwelling upon it. My only option was to pick myself up and remind myself what had attracted me to the job in the first place, even though it was going to be an uphill struggle that would be made more difficult by the fact of having to recruit a new team.

Most big transitions come without budget

What I hadn't initially realized was that I faced many more challenges besides the lack of personnel. Perhaps the biggest of these challenges was the gaping hole in RADAR's finances. The war chest that I had been counting on to help get us through the next stage was completely empty.

In the period between my predecessor leaving and me arriving, there had been an interim chief executive. I had asked him to give me the low-down on the situation at RADAR just before I joined. He had done his own financial due diligence early on and it had quickly become apparent that there was not enough cash in the system. By 'not enough cash' he meant that RADAR was three months away from being forced to close altogether. He'd not only had to conduct a massive redundancy programme, but had also had to go out to members to seek a further source of funding just to survive.

Whatever way you looked at it, RADAR faced a big challenge. We had no money, very few staff and a huge debt to pay. Fortunately, as I quickly discovered, I had a very supportive board who encouraged me to choose my own path from the off.

'Do it your way, and don't be burdened by history lessons,' they urged at our first formal meeting. 'Don't be over-shadowed by ghosts of the past and all the other strong characters that have come and gone.'

One of the RADAR board trustees, David Mills, whose 'day job' was as the CEO of the Post Office, immediately adopted an unofficial mentoring role, becoming another in a long line of impressive business leaders who have skilfully guided me over the years.

One of David's first pieces of advice was to get all of the bad news stories out there at the earliest opportunity. The second, which was connected to the first, was sort out the money problem. Thanks to the interim chief executive's sterling efforts, RADAR had £1 million of cash to tide it over. However, even with a flexible repayment plan in place, the debt put a strain on RADAR's already severely strained coffers. Plus, of course, when you have barely enough cash to survive, it is almost impossible to do anything dynamic, just at a time where dynamic action was very much required.

Creating new spirit and purposes to drive change

I got on with the task of working out 'what next' for RADAR. With so much to do, what would our strategy be? It would have been very easy to kick back and think: 'Well a lot of the agenda can be handed over to the new Disability Rights Commission. That is what it is there for.' We'd fought so hard to get a government commission and now was the time to let them get on with it.

There were two big reasons why that line of thinking didn't work for me. First, I have never been a kick-back-and-leave-things-to-others sort of person. I'd always erred firmly towards the if-the-job's-worth-doing camp. Second, it was going to take the DRC at least two or three years before it got fully up to speed. It needed to work out how the various processes it was mandated to do would work. For example, the DRC was authorized to carry out inquiries which could lead to organizations that failed to comply with the rules being placed under special measures. Similarly, they had power to organize class actions where, say, a number of businesses in one sector were all breaking the rules. In this case, they could prosecute them as one. Again though, the who, what, why and when still needed to be ironed out. Overall, the DRC had a long shopping list of powers, but hadn't yet got close to the stage of enacting any of them. If we hung around waiting for that to happen, we would lose valuable time and momentum. We still needed an active, viable and vocal disability movement in the meantime.

Even if the DRC miraculously leapt into action almost immediately, it was still always going to be an instrument of government. It had all of the baggage that impacted every quango, or third-party agency. The DRC would be constantly balancing their agenda between being strident in order to effect change, but not too strident for fear of upsetting the government or a key political donor, which would see them being hauled into the minister's office for a dressing down. These types of dressing downs are, of course, part and parcel of any organization seeking change, but the threat of funding cuts that frequently comes with them can be quite sobering. In my view, there was still a vacancy for an independent, savvy and testing lobby group.

I came up with a strategy called New Spirit at RADAR. The message behind it was all about supporting people with disability to feel much more energized about 'what next'. My goal was to encourage everyone to be much more active as citizens and to join the campaign for change. There was still much to be done and the issues at stake had an impact on so many individuals. Each election day, for example, we still encountered a situation where a good number of polling stations were completely inaccessible to disabled voters, something that should be beyond unacceptable in a functioning democracy. New Spirit at RADAR introduced a fresher, more modern campaign for change.

I followed the 'spirit' theme in rebuilding the team, looking for new recruits who really wanted to make a difference. My recruitment process was led by the search for individuals who wouldn't take no for an answer, many of whom were disabled. We put in place processes that gave everyone on the team much more say than they'd previously had in the organization. I also did my best to expose team members to the entire scope of what we were trying to do, which meant including them more in the parliamentary process.

Something that caught my eye very early on was RADAR's annual People of the Year awards scheme, which was a crucial part of our fundraising programme, bringing in a proportion of the £1 million a year funding we needed just to survive. The event, which culminated in a glitzy ceremony in December, rewarded individuals who had done 'good things' when it came to disability. My instinct was that, despite the all-important fundraising aspect, and the fact that I got to meet and get to know some fabulous people, the scheme had had its day. The criteria for winning an award didn't seem particularly robust, in fact, they felt a bit loose. At the first ceremony I attended, a man received an award for wrestling a knife off an attacker on a plane. This didn't seem to fit in with what I was trying to achieve with RADAR at all. It wasn't that I doubted the bravery or resilience of the award winners, it was simply that I felt the messages were packaged as 'inspiration porn' for non-disabled do-gooders.

The more I thought about it, the more I began to think that the awards summed up where RADAR was at that particular point. It had played a crucial role in securing the DDA, yet it had become stale. While the purpose of the New Spirit campaign was to move it towards becoming an organization known for having real bite, a bit like groups such as Stonewall or the Fawcett Society, the awards were contributing to holding that ideal back.

After mulling it over for a while, I came up with the idea of a 'human rights' awards scheme. We'd go back to first principles and completely revamp the awards scheme to give out meaningful awards to people who had changed things significantly. Even gaining a nomination required meeting a robust set of criteria and winning one would be even harder. Indeed, to be presented with a RADAR People of the Year award, you needed to be something else. The idea clearly resonated, because once it was launched we managed to obtain a good deal of sponsorship.

The gala dinner put a sharper focus on disability as a rights rather than a philanthropic issue

Within a few years, it became a well-established human rights awards scheme. The gala dinner became an annual fixture and company chief executives and ministers were always keen to attend. It put a sharper focus on disability as a rights rather than a philanthropic issue.

Risking political alienation

It couldn't all be about fundraising and rubbing shoulders with the great and the good. There was still a lot of

145

grass-roots campaigning required. One of key priorities for improving the original Disability Discrimination Act was to ensure people diagnosed with HIV, cancer and multiple sclerosis were included in the list of conditions covered by anti-discrimination legislation. RADAR lobbied hard to have those three impairments added into the Bill, and we worked closely with other campaigning organizations such as the Terrence Higgins Trust. It wasn't just a case of highlighting everything that had been left out of the legislation either. Now the 'fuss' had died down a little, it was becoming clear that certain things we'd been promised simply hadn't materialized. Many of the issues that had brought disabled campaigners out onto the streets years earlier had still not been resolved.

Thinking back to the remarkable achievements of the activists in the early 90s, it made sense to mobilize this strength of opinion once more. I alighted on the idea of a postcard campaign, where individuals would send pre-printed postcards to MPs, highlighting that promises X, Y and Z were not being met. This was something that was easy to do and highly effective. Each RADAR member would simply write a postcard, using the standard statements we provided them, and then send them off to their MP. The statements were written to be deliberately provocative, using phrasing such as 'there are millions of disabled people who still face these challenges' and that, despite the DDA, ministers were 'all but ignoring our plight'. To my absolute delight, the campaign just took off, practically taking on a life of its own. Before long, MPs were inundated with sacks full of postcards.

The UK Human Rights Commission: a pink blancmange of nothingness?

Despite its relative youth, the long-term prognosis for the DRC was not as positive. Just a few years into the DRC's tenure, a decision was taken to merge three commissions, Equal Opportunities, Disability Rights and Racial Equality into the new, multi-strand Equality and Human Rights Commission (EHRC). The new commission was established by the Equality Act 2006, and was intended to be the umbrella body for the enforcement and promotion of equality and non-discrimination laws in England, Scotland and Wales, harmonizing all previous legislation, while also taking responsibility for other aspects of equality such as age, sexual orientation and religion or belief. At the time, there was a whole range of what were then starting to be called 'protected characteristics' and it seemed to make sense to policymakers to bring them under one umbrella organization.

The merger was not something that was greeted with universal glee by many campaigners.

In the end, RADAR gave a reluctant nod of support to the EHRC, but like everyone else we had misgivings about it. I could see that the disability rights campaign would most likely find itself vastly disadvantaged as a smaller fish in a much larger organization.

I, like many others, had been so hopeful about the DRC, and about what could be done once it got into gear, but within a few years it collapsed into the pink blancmange I had been warned about.

Ultimately I was left with the feeling that governments don't always appreciate the differing challenges of various groups of people. It is hard not to think that with today's view that 'identity politics' need to be dismantled, this situation will only get worse. It certainly suggests that the success of commissions will only ever be as good as the quality of our parliamentary leaders' understanding of inequities.

Overall, it was all a huge disappointment. After all the campaigning and the perception that we were moving in the right direction, it felt like disability rights were no longer a priority for our government. In fact, they seemed a long way from it.

A lesson to learn: the change process is not linear

One of the most important learnings for me has been that change only feels slow at the time. It is only when you look back do you realize how time flies. However, the politics of change would be nowhere had it not been for the hard-won rights secured by those who were in front of us. Those that created a plan. Even if it isn't always linear.

Practical actions for employers and employees

For employers

MAP YOUR PROGRESS
Map out how far you have come by using one of the more reputable benchmark surveys such as that created by

Business Disability Forum (BDF). The Disability Smart Audit is a whole-organization disability management audit. It has been developed by BDF for many decades to help organizations measure and improve on performance for disabled customers, clients or service users, employees and stakeholders. It helps organizations to:

- gain an understanding in very practical terms of what 'good' looks like across an organization, what is and isn't working, and what they need to do in order to get it right
- recognize where an organization is doing well
- secure impartial, objective evidence to inform business improvement, and to enable organizations to allocate resources accordingly
- identify and minimize disability-related legal and reputational risk and provide tangible recommendations and solutions to enhance practice, policy and process within the organization

LOOK OUT FOR BIAS

As well as mapping out how far you have come, try also to notice the missiles that may be approaching six inches below the water line. 'Responsible tech' influencers including data scientist, AI (artificial intelligence) developers and HR leaders are increasingly seeking to address data biases built into AI recruitment tools. These champions care about avoiding discrimination based on gender, race or age – while still discriminating against these same diverse candidates who also happen to have a disability.

The debate on race and gender bias in AI-powered recruitment has already started but so far, disability is missing in that debate. Check out Disability Ethical A1 to find out more what you can do and to access resources.[1]

For employees

CONTRIBUTE TO SELECTION DECISIONS

Get inquisitive when it comes to supporting your employer to use reputable organizations that create the tools used to measure an organization's progress over time.

I listened in on an internal discussion with 20+ senior stakeholders from many geographies from a leading multinational. They were debating the relative merits of the different indexes, benchmark standards and audit tools available.

What impressed me the most was the high-quality attention the C-suite gave to listening to the feedback from employees heading up their global disability ERG.

This was truly an authentically led global strategy group that wanted to unpack the views of their own people. Do not think for one moment the options to influence do not exist.

BRING YOUR OWN CHAIR

That said, sometimes you will find it a hard slog to surface the lived experience of your fellow colleagues with disabilities. You won't always get a seat at the table. Though as one disability ERG leader infamously said, 'If you don't get a seat at the table, bring a folding chair.'

CHAPTER TEN

Getting *on* at work, rather than simply getting *in*

Channelling purpose

1 January 2006, and I awoke in the early hours of the morning feeling terrible. This wasn't down to any excesses from the New Year celebrations a few hours earlier. It was thanks to a feeling of dread around the one thought that kept going through my mind over and over: *I need to raise £1 million this year. Again.*

Of this much I was now certain: heading up NGOs was often about fundraising and that didn't interest me. It felt that everything we did at RADAR was geared to raising enough money to keep the machine going through the year in order to use it to lobby the government to do things they may, or may not, want to do.

I didn't want to do it any more. I like creating change and I'm not fond of raising the money to fund the instrument that sustains change.

I wanted to be playful, follow my nose and achieve things the way I thought they should be achieved, not through this endless cycle of fundraising, glad-handing and fighting for every minuscule step forward. There had to be a better and more effective way to make progress. If there wasn't, we'd still be doing the same things a decade from now and talking about the same issues. That just didn't make sense.

As I lay in bed, I went over some of the things I had done over the past year that weren't strictly RADAR business. Or, at least, the traditional business of raising money and then spending it on lobbying. As I had been doing since before I joined, I had focused on other sectors that had faced similar challenges, wondering if they had found more effective ways to move their campaigns forward. My attention returned to the fight for gender equality. During that time I kept reading about how companies were setting up employee networks for women and this struck a chord with me. Women used these platforms to speak to one another and, thanks to the momentum created by the growing scale of these networks, we had started to hear more about issues such as the gender pay gap. The battle wasn't won (indeed, it still isn't) but it was rising up the agenda.

It wasn't just the numbers game that made these groups successful though. It was because each of the members had skin in the game. These women's groups hadn't made breakthroughs because men had deigned to give them a break. They'd made progress because they were all so passionate about what they saw as obvious injustices because it was happening to them. They were at a disadvantage because of their gender, something they had no control over. No wonder they had the strength to rise up and call for change. Movements happen when people get together and say: *No more. Not in my name.* It is this groundswell of passion that makes things happen.

Movements happen when people get together and say: No more. Not in my name

For as long as I could remember, I had been asking myself what it was, strategically, that I should be doing to make that big, all-important step-change for people with disability, to ensure that their rights are secured. I had long since decided that the obvious place to begin was the workplace, where people in paid employment were cheesed off because they hadn't got the workplace adjustments they needed, or who felt marginalized or ignored, or even belittled. What, for example, could be done to give people in employment more security? When it comes to jobs it should not just be about *getting in*, it should also be about *getting on*. Work is such an important part of our lives and a huge privilege. People who have jobs are more likely to build resilience against other human experiences that can derail us, whether it is health conditions, poverty or depression. They live more engaged lives.

Despite the legislation and the introduction of the DRC and then EHRC, people with disability were still the least employed and most likely to experience poverty, or less quality in terms of healthcare. They still had more challenges in terms of housing and were less likely to get the transport they need. We needed to find a way to ensure more people with disability not only got into the workplace, but also found a way up the greasy pole, to the next position up and then the next position up from there. It occurred to me that the women's network concept could translate very well to what I wanted to do. What they'd started to achieve translated very well to where we needed to be when it came to working together to improve the rights of employees with disability in the workplace. We needed everyone who is affected by the injustices that we've heard about time and again to stand together and call for change.

Disability employee resource groups/networks: a new eco-system

One of my favourite expressions is: when you've been lying in the ditch too long, it gets comfortable down there. It might feel a bit damp, but it's safe and its familiar.

The time had now come when people needed to be bold, loud and proud

Why try to climb out? For too long, this had been the case with disability rights in the workplace. For many, it just seemed like such a big leap to say: No more, not in my name. But the time had now come when people needed to be encouraged to share their stories with one another and be bold, loud and proud. How irresistible would that be? We needed to harness that passion for change and disability networks were the way to do it.

Excited by the idea, I resolved to start looking around to see if anything was already being done in this direction. The answer was yes, but not a lot. A handful of large organizations, such as BT, Royal Bank of Scotland and Lloyds Banking Group had given their employees with disability the green light to set up ad hoc groups. This seemed like a good place to start, so I got in touch with each company and said: Can I come and see you and hear about what you are doing? Each organization invited me in and were very welcoming, but what they told me was not encouraging.

'They are not very well organized,' I was told. 'The big problem is most employees don't really want to be associated with a disability resource group or network.'

Even though the early signs were not good, my gut instinct told me that the way forward was in creating really meaningful, sophisticated conversations between all the employees with a disability within a company; conversations they wanted to be part of. Even better, create a dialogue between disability networks across companies. This was the way to build a new movement: strength in numbers, just as they were doing in the fight for gender equality.

Despite their early teething troubles, there were lessons to be learnt from the ad hoc disability resource groups and networks that had already appeared. The biggest issue, as I had been warned, was that they weren't very well organized. Many of them began after some more imaginative organizations saw the value in gender networks and threw a bit of budget at someone, telling them to do the same for employees with disability. Most of the time though, the individuals charged with putting it all together were not particularly senior and therefore lacked the knowledge to do anything meaningful. This haphazard approach had the knock-on effect that efforts to set up disability networks were often viewed with scepticism by diversity and inclusion teams.

The more I thought about it, the more convinced I became that there was a way to make this work. In fact, I became incredibly excited about the potential of disability employee resource groups (ERGs) and decided that it was up to *me* to make this happen. This was exactly where my talents lay. I didn't want to be running around trying to raise cash. I would far rather use my skills to persuade business leaders to back ERGs in their organizations. If we all got behind this idea, things would change much, much more quickly than if we held another black-tie awards do and listened to a few rousing speeches while drinking lukewarm champagne. I would never be able to achieve this within RADAR though. It was not something I could run concurrently with my CEO role.

I had come to another crossroads in my life. The choice was simple: continue as CEO at RADAR, or set up my own, boutique consultancy, put my money where my mouth was and make the concept of ERGs a reality. The second option was nerve-wracking. It certainly wasn't the easier option. It would take time to work with individual companies to set up their own ERGs and then even more time to bring the various networks together, so they could cooperate and use their numbers to encourage meaningful change.

Was there a middle ground? I could go to another organization and use all that I had learnt in a different role. I had a good reputation in the industry and already had five years in a top job under my belt. Even as I weighed it up, I knew I wouldn't be happy somewhere else. What were the other alternatives? Over the years, numerous people had asked me why I hadn't become an MP, to help force change from within the political arena. It seemed logical: I knew my way around Westminster and had some good contacts among parliamentarians. It was a possibility, but in reality this would have been even tougher than setting out alone. In order to make a mark in politics, you need to start out when you are a lot younger, certainly by your early thirties. I had already missed that train.

There was something else too. On a personal level, I needed to move on. I had worked and worked and worked since leaving university. I had always been so driven and obsessed with doing well and moving beyond that 'little job'. Now I stepped back and looked at my career, on the brink of making a massive change. I had not long been divorced, a very amicable and mutually agreed ending to a marriage to a great man. I was not actively looking for a significant other, I knew there was no real chance of finding them while toiling away at a CEO role, whether at RADAR or elsewhere. In my time at RADAR, I had been fortunate enough to work under two brilliant chairs. Before that, I had got to know some incredible and dynamic chief executives such as Susan Scott-Parker and Richard Gutch. Yet one thing they all had in common was that they took work very seriously indeed. I still wanted to do well, but I wanted to have enough space to breathe and enjoy my life too. I wanted to enjoy the ride.

Leaving RADAR to set up on my own would be a big step. There would be people who would accuse me of playing Russian roulette with my career. I was, after all, at the top of my profession as far as the NGO sector went. I was paid well too. Yes, my salary wasn't as much as I'd receive in the corporate sector, but it was substantial. I had a wardrobe full of nice clothes, often ate at some of the best restaurants and led a very comfortable life indeed. Yet something big was missing. That something was the contribution I wanted to make to the world.

As I thought about shaking-up my life and turning everything I knew upside down, I was reminded of a quote I had read in *Body and Soul: How to succeed in business and change the world*, a book by Body Shop entrepreneur Anita Roddick.[1] She had written that it was our duty to endeavour to be anything, *anything*, in life, but just not to be mediocre. I was satisfied that what I was imagining now was about as far from mediocre as it can get. It was time to make the break.

Finding perspective

I gave the RADAR board six months' notice but ended up working nearly a year. It takes a long time to hire a successor to a senior role and I was happy to give them the flexibility. There was a big temptation to jump in and get started right away as soon as I left, but I knew I needed a break. I'd been working long hours at RADAR and needed to rest before my next work adventure.

As I worked my final few months at RADAR, I didn't have much time to reflect on what I had achieved to date. We were deeply involved in the organization of the next People of the Year awards scheme. If I had so reflected, the question I would most likely have asked myself was: What did I make happen during my five and a half years there? The most obvious proof of success was that the place still existed. When I arrived we'd been almost out of money. The organization had changed and had a bit more verve about it and had adopted a more modern approach. Was it going to change the world though? Not with me. My skills were not what it needed. On a personal level, my contribution was rewarded with an OBE for 'services to disabled people', which I acknowledged as recognition. I have never been one to quite know how to take any personal praise or the honours system, but in the end, I was quite moved to be awarded it.

A lesson to learn: fear can make us deeply intentional

Navigating disability and making sense of a new identity often means confronting fear. Sometimes that can make you brittle. And sometimes it can make you deeply purposeful and intentional in how you live your life. But first, you often need an employer to give you a break.

Navigating disability and making sense of a new identity often means confronting fear

James Partridge recounts in *Face It*, his wonderful last book

159

before he died in 2021, the story of his job interview for a research assistant in health economics at St Thomas' Hospitals Community Medicine Department in the University of London.[2] It was June 1976. Five years previously he had experienced a road traffic accident that had left him with life-changing facial disfigurement. He experienced years going in and out of hospital having numerous surgeries, all while studying at Oxford University. He recounts the interview with five people on the panel. Question after question. And then the stinger question: 'I see you've had quite a lot of plastic surgery, Mr Partridge. Do you think you'll be needing some more?' James steels himself and keeps calm. He explains in a few sentences that he had not had any surgery for two years. And then, unable to control himself he asks, 'Do you think I need some more?' As soon as the words left his lips, he regretted it. He saw the panel recoil. He was ushered out the room.

Two days later the letter came. He got the job. He got the career break he wanted.

While the sentence was not rehearsed and 'judicious use of sarcasm' not a deliberate tactic in this case, it did the trick for James.

Twenty years or so later when he was chief executive of Changing Faces, the organization he founded, I met him for the first time. I was deputy chief executive of Arthritis Care. I was at his offices and in the reception area. He was running late from another appointment and bounded in from the street. His receptionist explained he is late and had kept me waiting. He turned and first spotted a small boy looking at some leaflets on inner confidence alongside lots of literature on show. He crouched behind him and reached out to a specific pamphlet. He took it from the shelves and placed it into the hands of the boy. Boy and adult turned to look at each other. Their faces mirrored each other. The look on the boy's face was incredulous on seeing 'someone like him' and being witness to that private moment has never left me. I wonder even now how the boy grew up, where he works, what he does, how he lives his life and whether that moment remains as important to him as to me, a spectator watching a leader in flow.

James's fear all those years ago in front of an important job panel had been channelled for decades and this man was working to purpose and with intent. Fear can make you deeply intentional to help those that come behind us.

Practical actions for employers and employees

For employers

FIND YOUR COMMUNITY

Look in different places to find a community of extraordinary purple talent. Make a beeline for the Shaw 100 Power List which is published each year.

The annual Shaw Trust Disability Power 100 celebrates the most influential disabled people in the UK, nominated by the public and judged by an independent panel. Nationally and internationally recognized, it is the only campaign that shines a light on disabled people at the top of their game and in positions of influence across all sectors of society. Shaw Trust showcases the capabilities and strengths of disabled people to shatter negative perceptions of disability and expose the benefits of accessibility and inclusion.

It is worth getting involved, nominating your own people and certainly demonstrating you are an ally by cascading the results.

STUDY THE VALUABLE 500

If you want to be at the top of your game notice how 20 per cent of the Valuable 500 companies, *as they signed up*, mentioned they are looking to set up, or have already set up, a disability ERG as part of their commitment.

While I would applaud these public statements it is worth noting that they were made by the very chief executives and C-suite leaders who, by joining Valuable 500, were agreeing to make ONE COMMITMENT. Some 20 per cent of those leaders had decided that learning directly from their own people, via the establishment of a disability ERG, was the most important strategic decision they needed to make.

I would like, one day, to hear what each of them has learnt. The quality of their learning and the actions that follow will be in direct proportion to their listening.

For employees

SEEK OUT THE FEARLESS STORYTELLERS

We all learn by watching, noting and observing others. You will learn a huge amount by constantly seeking out the ways in which people with disabilities share their story of difference.

When James Partridge and I used to meet for lunch he would often muse on our role as perpetual storytellers. We would debate the role and value of storytelling as a mechanism for change.

Now, as I look back, I notice the reticence I had in being labelled a storyteller. Brene Brown did a wonderful TED Talk about the moment an event planner asked her if they could refer to her as a storyteller on the event flyer.[3] The event manager didn't want to refer to her as a researcher as that would deem her 'boring and irrelevant' but on the suggestion to call Brene a storyteller she was shocked. The academic in her was worried, her reaction was, 'Why not call me magic pixie!'

The point being, seek them out. Their experiences, techniques, tricks and flicks will help you build the brand you want for yourself.

After all, as Brene says, stories are just data with a soul.

READ SOPHIE
Read Sophie Morgan's book, *Driving Forward*. Carpe that f*****g Diem. It will make sense when you read the book. Just do it.[4]

CHAPTER ELEVEN

Starting a long-haul strategy to change the world

With no money, where do you start?

The odds of success for any new business are not promising. Statistics vary, but it is believed that 20 per cent of small businesses don't see their first birthday, 30 per cent don't see their second and half of new businesses fail within five years.[1] The statistics don't break down to reveal the number of entrepreneurial ventures set up by people with disabilities, but I suspect the numbers are quite small. Certainly, the presence of organizations such as The Prince's Trust and Kaleidoscope Investments, which support people with disabilities to become successful entrepreneurs, seems to indicate that it is a relatively unusual phenomenon.

I was in the position of not only trying to get an untested idea onto the market, but I was also launching in the face of an economic downturn. In the spring of 2007, the markets were already awash with rumours of tough times ahead. It would have been easy to feel discouraged. I certainly had a few anxieties about whether or not the venture would be a success and what I would live on.

I had taken a long four-month holiday after leaving RADAR. I had barely touched my phone during the holiday because I was determined to have a proper break from it all.

Picking up the phone on my return, I had a call from Susan Scott-Parker of the Business Disability Forum (BDF) who offered me some project work.

The task itself turned out to be quite meaty. Susan wanted me to write an engagement strategy for BDF, in response to the organization beginning to lose some of its top-tier (and top-paying) partners. The organization needed a high-level engagement strategy. We agreed a six-month consultancy contract to deliver the strategy. It couldn't have worked out better for me. Not only would I be supporting an organization that really matters; I would also have a source of income and have time to set up my own separate business with a completely different purpose.

Once I arrived back in London, the HQ of Kate Nash Associates was established in the corner of my small flat in Tanner Street, just off Bermondsey Street. But my priority was to get out and speak with as many people as I possibly could, while simultaneously working on a disability ERG best practice guide.

It would, of course, have been lovely to solely focus on the best practice paper, but since its purpose was to make a very big impression with a manifesto for change, opening up the conversation about the need for a series of employment resource groups (ERGs), I also needed to build up my contacts in business and pave the way for what I was up to.

It wasn't long before my days filled up with meetings and I got into an exhausting routine of going out to press the flesh and spread the word and then return to my flat to further agonize over my publication. I knew what I wanted to do and say, but nevertheless found it quite hard to write. This was the first attempt to create a series of networks like this, so a lot of what I was writing was purely theoretical. I was convinced that this was an important, indeed essential, step forward but I had no solid evidence to support my supposition that delivering high-quality disability ERGs would be embraced by employers or employees. This made writing a convincing and compelling call-to-action quite difficult.

If you don't ask, you don't get

After drafting and redrafting the publication a few more times, I finally decided I needed to just get it out there and let the stakeholders decide on my 10-point plan to set up and run ERGs. I now needed to make good on all the expressions of support and set up as high-profile an event as I could muster.

Asking organizations for money is never easy. Something that I found quite quickly is that now I was asking for something concrete, it became a bit more of a struggle to engage people than when you are talking about an idea. Also, it's a lot easier to ask when you are the CEO of a large organization, rather than a one-person consultancy.

If you're in this position, you'll find that many doors that were previously open will be quietly closed. Fortunately, that wasn't the case with every door. One of my first, and arguably most useful, expressions of support came from the late Lord Jack Ashley. It was perhaps no surprise that he quickly got behind the publication. Jack, who was deaf himself, had always been a tireless campaigner for the issues he cared about and most of those issues centred around disability. I approached him and was completely honest about the fact I was now working on my own, without the might of an organization behind me. To his credit, he agreed to help straight away.

Jack Ashley's willingness to write a message of endorsement for the publication meant that others were immediately more open to the idea.

My next big breakthrough was with John Varley, the CEO of Barclays Bank. I had long been an admirer of his. He had a powerful sense of justice. He always wanted the best for his team. Every year he would hold listening groups for Barclays' employees with a disability, which he would personally chair. He would ask everyone what was working well and what were the missiles six inches below the surface that he knew nothing about. Most importantly, he would listen carefully to the answers and, if anything was not going as planned, he would take steps to correct it.

Leaders who see the business benefits recognize they have to invest in the tools

I was, of course, delighted, although not for the first time realized that passionate CEOs and C-suite leaders who see the business benefits of employing people with disabilities sometimes recognize they have to invest in the tools that will help their organizations to get it right.

I then secured support from BT, Citibank, Direct Enquiries, the Equality and Human Rights Commission, Ernst & Young, GlaxoSmithKline, Lloyds TSB and Motability Operations. It was enough to get the material published and printed. There was just one more challenge: how and where to launch it. It did all feel like a bit of a one-shot deal. I had put all this effort into the publication and now it had to make maximum impact.

I spoke with Sally Ward, the Inclusion Specialist at BT, whom I'd known for many years. Her early support was so central to the idea of setting up a network of networks.

I suggested that she might be able to offer us a space at one of their training sites, or perhaps even something somewhere in the corporate HQ. 'I think we can go one better than that,' she replied. 'How about the BT Tower?'

The was better than all my expectations. The BT Tower in Fitzrovia is one of London's most iconic buildings. Most corporate executives would jump at the chance of going to an event there. It was perfect.

Becoming a Networkologist

My first year of going solo had been all about getting the publication out. It was going to be both my calling card and the vehicle that would get the idea of the ERG networks out there, legitimize what I was doing and start the dialogue. Even though the launch event had been a huge success, I was under no illusions that this was going to be an easy job. In the discussions I had had, I had already come across people who were doubtful that the idea would work. Some even dismissed it outright as patronizing, or felt disability ERGs could never be as powerful as gender networks which were led by kick-ass women who really did know how to have difficult conversations with chief executives about the gender pay gap. Another of the most frequent rejoinders had been that people with arthritis have nothing in common with those who are deaf or hard of hearing, or who have multiple sclerosis. They completely missed the point that it was not about the *specifics* of the impairment, but about the *common barriers* that we all face in the workplace.

It was not about the specifics of the impairment, but about the common barriers that we all face

Branding was, I decided, the key to getting organizations to at least be intrigued enough by the idea to start the conversation. As long as you get the core product right and deliver it well, a strong brand will sell and sell. After spending so long understanding what a disability ERG might look like and firming up my ideas via the publication, I needed to take the idea to a wider audience. To do this, I had to inspire and intrigue people. That is how I came up with the concept of 'Networkology'. It was quirky, catchy and seemed to neatly sum up the result I wanted. To spread the word, I added the signature 'Kate Nash, chief Networkologist' to all my emails.

'What on earth is a Networkologist?'

'Well, I create networks.'

And I'd be off. After a while it caught on. I'd be at an event and people would introduce me by saying: Have you met Kate Nash? She's a Networkologist…

And there it was; another opportunity to spread the word. Before long, Networkology became a natural part of my brand. Most importantly, I was getting the idea of disability ERGs talked about.

Once I got my foot in the door, I would come right out with it.

'You have a fantastic gender network, an amazing LGBT+ network and your BAME network is cooking on gas. Let's see if there is a case for a disability network.'

Disability ERGs/networks: let them get on with it

I had imagined that most of my work would come from local authorities, universities and the NHS, but in fact most of the interest came from the private sector.

Perhaps true to their type, they were more entrepreneurial and willing to try something new, tweak it and then try it again. But both sectors were interested.

Invariably, talking to the right person meant tapping into their enthusiasm to speed up change. That would drive energy which then surged through the entire organization. Very often, what fuelled the switch was the point when someone within the focus groups took up the mantle to lead the disability ERG/network. Nine times out of 10, the leader was not an obvious choice but then when I heard their story it was quite clear exactly why they were the right person. They would either have a disability themselves, or an ally, such as a parent, spouse or a child with a disability. After a while, I found that, somehow, I could spot at 20 paces someone with an important ally story. It was uncanny. I'd always make a beeline for them and ask straight out: Why do you want to be a disability champion? Nearly every time I would be rewarded with a direct, or indirect, story of an experience of disability and I'd know that I had found my network leader. If I pitched it right, someone would get passionate about it. There would be the person who would want to lead, who would bring together a few others to have a pilot Networkology workshop.

Not all organizations were the same. Some would undertake much of the work themselves, while others would invite me in to hold workshops to point them in the right direction, so their own diversity teams could then set up disability ERGs/networks. Others wanted more hands-on help to speed up change.

Occasionally, I would be asked to be a mentor or coach to the person leading the network. There were a variety of strategies which we developed over time, from toolkits to help share learning, to a deep dive on workplace adjustment aspect to see what was working, or not. Once networks were established there was occasionally a piece of remedial work to be done to ensure they stayed fully aligned with the main organization and maintained a shared agenda.

The business built steadily, with me managing up to a dozen clients a month. Once the network was successfully running I went on to the next one, leaving the teams to get on with it. Often, I would be asked to go back to do a keynote address, particularly on 3 December, the International Day of Persons with Disabilities, which was always a bit of juggle. As time went on, I'd frequently have to turn down requests because I was already booked.

It was, of course, tougher to get it across the line in some organizations than others. It was always quite difficult if anyone had tried to set up some sort of disability ERG/network before but got zero response. After a little gentle probing it would emerge that a disability inclusion lead would have put the bare bones of a network in place with the best of intentions but failed to generate the necessary excitement or interest for it to get any traction. Often, this was partly because the initiators did not experience disability themselves. Experience told me that this made it incredibly tough to set up the ERGs/networks. It was just too difficult to tap into what the potential issues were. Yes, they knew the policy practice procedure to the letter but that didn't necessarily lead straight on to a complete understanding of the lack of self-confidence and self-worth that plagues many disabled people.

In the early days I wanted to be quite strategic about the business I took on. The reality was, like all small businesses, I took on whatever work I was offered! The good news was it was heading in the right direction. Disability ERGs/networks were here to stay.

A lesson to learn: this social media land is ours

When I look back to my college years and the early days of seeking work, I realize that there was a dearth of disabled role models in my life. In fact, there was no one in my life who had the same experiences as I did when I was first trying to secure my first job.

This is why when I see young disabled influencers, I just can't help but shout 'go forth young people!' There was no such thing as Twitter, Facebook, Instagram in my day.

There was a dearth of disabled role models in my life

In his BBC online article in 2021, Johny Cassidy showcases some of the most success-ful disabled influencers making their mark on social media.[2] He profiles Tess Daly with 200,000+ followers on Instagram. She uses her platform to promote her beauty tutorials and advertise beauty brands. She is an electric wheelchair user who has spinal muscular atrophy and has worked on social marketing campaigns for Boohoo and Pretty Little Thing. At just 32 at the time of the BBC article Tess cringes at the term 'social influencer' and wishes there were more people like her when she was growing up.

Bernadette Hagans has 28,000+ followers on Instagram. She is Northern Irish and an amputee model. In 2020 she started working with luxury shoe brand Kurt Geiger. One post from her may get over 1,500 likes. She stares pro-vocatively at the camera armed with youth, beauty and an artificial leg, daring us not to part with a lot of money for glorious shoes.

Kurt Geiger's chief executive, Neil Clifford, believes the rise in disabled influencers is down to the public change of mood. He says:

> The boom in social media has given a voice to those who have previously been underrepresented in the public eye,

and they are, quite rightly, demanding to be seen and heard. People expect businesses to utilize their influence to counter inequality and many brands are reacting to this need.

And then there is blogger Pippa Stacey who lives with chronic fatigue syndrome. She shares how her content outperformed other non-disabled influencers. She partnered with the supermarket chain Tesco to profile their Easy Bake recipes, showing how the recipes enabled her to pace herself. She hopes it encourages Tesco and others to work with more diverse influencers in the future. I look up the recipes myself.

Practical actions for employers and employees

For employers

CHECK OUT SOCIAL MEDIA INFLUENCERS

Even if you cannot convince your employer to use disabled social influencers, it is worth examining their work as well as researching the impact they are having on the brands of others.

While it is good to see how brands are noticing the opportunity for innovation, not to mention a simple case of wanting to get a slice of the $8 trillion market (the purple pound/dollar/yuan), it is equally good to see people with disabilities using social media as a force for good, for their own purposes. And no matter how you look at it they are sassy 'take-no-prisoners' and out, loud and proud. Whether they are trying to, or not, they are paying it forward. They are helping disabled people that come behind us. They take the term 'fearless' to a new level. I sure hope they are being paid as much as any other non-disabled social influencer that help brands to make more sales.

SET UP A BURSARY

If you want to support other young new entrants to the market, why not simply set up a prestigious bursary scheme for young disabled graduates who want a career in social media and communications. Be prepared to fund the extra costs of volunteering that may come and ensure you have an end-to-end programme that enables someone to get that 'first shot' at a paid job later down the line.

For employees

BECOME THE LYNCHPIN

Throughout my career, whether I did it consciously, or not, I suppose I have always tried to be the lynchpin. To try and be indispensable. I suppose I figured that if I was someone an employer didn't want to get rid of, or even a consultant they didn't want to get rid of, well, I would work forever. It can come at a cost but mostly, if you get the balance right, it can be a hugely important part of your brand. It doesn't have to mean working harder. It's about working on the right things and putting your employer first. After all, they are paying you.

SLEEP MORE

It sounds trite but if I had a dollar for every time I have heard an employee with disability talk about burnout born by tiredness, I would be a rich woman indeed. And this does not contradict the suggestion to be a lynchpin.

John Amaechi, in his book *The Promises of Giants*, says, 'Do not sleep on the importance of sleep! It is our final factor and a bedrock for resilience. No one is programmed to be an optimal performer with fewer than six hours of quality sleep.'[3]

For some of us it's more.

CHAPTER TWELVE

The third phase of change

When movements take off

Forget the numbers game

Something that I noticed very quickly is that my opening discussions about ERGs/networks mostly took on a familiar pattern. They would normally begin with me being invited in by the diversity and inclusion team who had heard about my successes with other disability ERGs. Generally, I would be asked to lead a focus group with a small number of employees with a disability which would mainly be an information gathering exercise addressing the challenges behind setting up a network. There seemed to be one major stumbling block and it came up time and again.

'We don't have enough disabled people to warrant a network,' the group would say.

'Yes, you have,' I'd respond. 'If you look up the figures from the Office for National Statistics, or the Department of Work and Pensions, or other government sources, you will see that every organization, of any size, in any geography, or any jurisdiction has around 10 per cent. In the public sector, that figure is nearer 12 per cent.'

This would always be the cue for much shaking of heads.

'No, no, we've done our monitoring and the figure here is 1 per cent.'

'Nope, you've got 10 per cent.'

Why the disparity in the figures? The somewhat depressing answer was that most people didn't feel able to share information about their disability via the formal monitoring processes. A large part of this is down to a question of trust. If organizations didn't create that environment of trust, people would not come forward. Plus, after years of being confronted with hostile language such as 'disclose' and 'declare' it seemed like a very big deal indeed to step forward and say: *I have X condition, and it might affect my job in Y way. However, with a little adjustment, I can do everything I am employed to do.*

John Amaechi, the former basketball player turned psychologist, has a great take on this. John, who was the first NBA player to come out publicly and who has since become one of the world's most high-profile gay athletes, had, perhaps understandably, some powerful words about trusting others with highly personal information.

'Information is a gift,' he told me. 'We always think it is all about ourselves when we share personal information, but if you are the recipient of that information, it means you have created enough trust for people to give you that gift.'

I could not have put it any better. For ERGs to be truly effective we needed to work together to create an environment where people felt comfortable giving the gift of information that was so personal to them.

There is no big answer to the right way to set up a successful disability ERG/network, but it starts with persuading the 10 per cent in each company that they have a role to play in these networks. We all have a duty to step up. Key to this is creating the environment where the 10 per cent feel comfortable in having what could seem like a difficult conversation and giving the gift of their story. As I found myself repeatedly articulating my views on the best ways to build personal resilience and help move things in the right direction, I began to wonder if there was any merit in getting it all down on paper. I was, after all, saying broadly similar things to every company I visited. The idea began to form to write a book, which could convey the message to both employees with a disability and their employers, so everyone got the maximum benefit out of disability ERGs/networks. As so often happens, I didn't really give enough thought to what a big challenge writing a book was, particularly when I was already working long days, but by then I was committed.

Secrets & Big News

The core idea behind my first book, *Secrets & Big News*, was to answer the question about why it was so hard to share personal information about disability and to highlight what employers and colleagues can do to support their teams in working through this dynamic.[1] It's not my intention to push this book here, but in it I wanted to develop the theme of the soft bigotry of low expectations and the impact this can have on people. In the book I also put forward constructive suggestions about the right way for employers to approach the issue of listening in a sensitive yet positive way. I knew first-hand the extreme frustration experienced by the regular intrusion of well-meaning people who often immediately assume that the number one goal for anyone with a disability is to get better when they have absolutely no choice about their situation

Well-meaning people often assume that the number one goal for anyone with a disability is to get better

and there is no cure. (Note to anyone reading this: don't *ever* ask me if I have tried copper bracelets. I genuinely don't care if they worked for your Aunt Doris and eased her pain. Apologies if this sounds blunt: judicious sarcasm doesn't work so well on the printed page!)

I put together an editorial advisory board to help me with the research. The board was made up of people who had supported what I had been doing for years. I also secured the agreement of 55 employer partners who rolled out the survey, and between them engaged 2,511 disabled employees who agreed to take part in our research project. The goal of the research was to discover the key barriers to employees sharing personal information about disability and to answer the question as to why those with disabilities were not always willing to describe themselves as disabled, let alone share their story. I was also curious about what it was that employers were doing (or not doing) that was perhaps adding to this reticence. Were their monitoring processes too much of a blunt instrument that had the opposite effect of what they wanted to achieve?

The very strong message that came back was that while policy and practice played a part in the disconnect, it was much more about confidence. Those organizations that had been successful in opening a dialogue identified story-telling as the key to break through any difficulties getting everyone to connect. Many of the networks that had already been set up had made huge progress via story-telling campaigns. It seemed an obvious theme to develop, both within the book and elsewhere.

The findings confirmed a lot of what I had already surmised. There is something very important about being able to protect your brand as a high performing individual at the same time as being able to share your story. I don't mean in the big platform moments, even though they are extremely powerful for anyone who is a good orator and are a great way to spread the word. I mean sharing your story on a day-to-day basis. Take as an example a person who has a lower-back condition, or repetitive strain injury (RSI), or who has mobility issues following a stroke. This individual is standing by the photocopier, getting on with their work, when a colleague asks them if they can help out by bringing through a tray of cups of tea to the meeting room. In the past, the person with a disability may well have made a vague excuse and made an awkward exit to extract themselves from the situation. They'd most likely beat themselves up about the embarrassment of it all for the rest of the day. This situation will be repeated again and again throughout their working life if they don't change it. It will most likely lead to them doing anything they can to remain low key, which includes not pushing themselves forward and going for promotion. In an ideal world, they would be brave enough to say, 'Apologies, I regret that I can't do that because of my RSI.' (And there only needs to be one apology. There is no need to go on apologizing. One is not apologizing for having RSI; one is apologizing that on that occasion, and for that ask, they cannot help.) Story told. Job done. Get on with the day job and shine.

This will never happen though unless people learn to tell their story. The inability to share a small piece of very necessary information blights too many people's lives. Telling that story changes everything.

I've seen numerous examples of how powerful this can be. One of my inspirations is Amanda Rowland, who has a visual impairment and who was a partner at PwC until her retirement. She shared how she was deliberately always very direct. When her colleagues put up a PowerPoint during a meeting she'd immediately call them out, saying something like: 'I have told you before, I can't see this.' She was always acutely aware that junior consultants in the same position who were climbing the greasy pole wouldn't have the confidence to raise the issue. It was far more likely they'd sit in silence and potentially be disadvantaged by not having access to a key part of the discussion. It was, she said, the reason that she always made a big point of reminding everyone in the room. Not in a hectoring way – but from a place of confidence, humour and expectation. PwC now have a very mature ERG network called DAWN. I am sure that is a great deal down to Amanda's senior executive sponsorship and personal experience in those early days.

It takes a lot of practice to tell your story with strength. When you first articulate your story, it takes a huge amount of courage. That can be especially so if you are telling it to someone who means everything to you.

My specific story relates to when I was in a new relationship with my partner Mark. I was some weeks into the relationship before I said anything about arthritis at all. He'd been on a visit to London and was just about to leave for Bahrain when I decided I had to say something. He looked stricken when I told him I really needed to speak to him before he left. He nearly laughed with relief when I told him I had arthritis.

When you first articulate your story, it takes a huge amount of courage

'I know,' he said. He made it easy to be me.

The point being that arthritis has had a big impact not just in terms of how I see the world but also on many other things such as how I look, how I move, how I walk, how I get out of a car or sit on a chair. These things I will always struggle with but find hard to articulate. Sometimes you need to have the difficult conversations in order to have the best conversations. I'd rather not have had to speak so openly about things that were distressing, but it was such an important part of my life that I needed to.

What are the truths in your story?

I always tell people with a disability that when you have not told your story before, it doesn't come easily. In fact, it can be excruciating. You didn't want to look and feel like that. When you do manage to say it, the words may not come out as you'd want them too. It may even make you a little emotional. You may even cry. Other people's reaction could well make things worse, because you don't want sympathy or pity (who does?). It is not their fault. We are flawed as human beings and don't necessarily know how to deal with the lived experiences of others. Even so, it can make the storyteller more prickly, angry or upset. Over time, with the telling and the retelling, it will get easier and people build inner confidence. This amazing act will make it easier for all those who follow us too.

As well as developing the theme of storytelling, *Secrets & Big News* offered 15 'big ideas' that both employers and employees could try. For employers, it was about helping them become more informed so they could help their team manage their journey and tell their story. This would frequently involve making changes such as ditching out-dated language such as 'disclose' and 'declare' in a move towards the far more inviting process of 'sharing'. I also suggested that we refrain from labelling workplace adjustment processes as the 'reasonable' adjustment/accommodation process, which strongly hints that such changes are a potential burden and move towards the more engaging 'workplace adjustments/accommodations'. For employees, the big ideas were based around taking a new and different approach and building their confidence to do so. In addition to storytelling, I urged them to get involved in disability ERGs/networks, which were already proving to be effective and to be sure to provide positive feedback to their employer.

Celebrating purple talent

I couldn't help thinking that to build a disability move-ment within the employers' community we needed to think carefully about brand. I was advocating big changes, yet we were still so strongly linked to the language of the past. Far too many of the disability ERGs/networks I'd worked with had tied themselves in knots trying to be too clever with the word 'disability', rather than focus on the drivers that lead to change.

The term 'purple pound' had been gaining traction ever since a news feature on BBC Ouch (a website and podcast series that reflects the lives and experiences of disabled people) in 2011 which talked about the spending power of disabled people.[2] Perhaps there was an opportunity to develop this concept. My thought process turned to the trend of movements adopting a colour as a shorthand, hence grey indicated the older community, rainbow said LGBT and green signified environmental issues.

Adopting purple as 'our' brand would offer a strong, simple way to denote the value of disabled talent

Adopting purple as 'our' brand would perhaps offer a strong, yet simple, way to denote the value of disabled talent, avoiding the need for employers to navigate their way around the minefield of trying to use the 'right' language when talking with their employees.

'Could there be any merit in using the phrase purple talent?' I wrote at the end of *Secrets & Big News*. 'Should we now create purple networks across the business and public sector?'

I asked this question in early April 2014 and the re-action was instant. In a matter of weeks, I was inundated with emails saying the 15 Big Ideas I had written it around had really struck a chord. People started discussing and debating it on LinkedIn and I was invited to speak at events run by all sorts of organizations, many of which I'd had no previous contact with.

News about my work with networks spread further afield too. Suzanne Colbert got in touch with me. She led the equivalent of Business Disability Forum (BDF) in Australia, having set up the Australian Network on Disability in the year 2000, and was keen to find a way to collaborate. After our conversation, I went out to Sydney to speak at the Australian Network on Disability's annual conference, and then spent some time there afterwards delivering training sessions to their members.

This was not my only foray into international waters. KPMG approached me after the consultancy had been awarded a contract with the employment minister in Saudi Arabia. The minister was keen to explore the barriers to working better with employees with disability and any blocks they might be facing. I was asked to contribute to the scoping exercise they were involved with and this led to a number of trips back and forth to Saudi. The collaboration, in turn, prompted the launch of Qaderoon, a Saudi-led business disability network, another important international ally.

A global network of disability ERGs/networks

It was soon clear that things had moved on a stage and the number of disability ERGs/networks began to swell at a rapid and very pleasing rate. Once enough organizations had set up their own disability ERGs/networks, the idea began to gain a momentum of its own. The manifestation of this was that many ERGs wanted to connect with other groups at other organizations. The networks wanted to be networked to share best practice and help one another make even more of a difference. I was, it seemed, the perfect person at the centre of it all that could facilitate this.

It took a while for me to realize that I was quietly playing cupid between organizations. I would receive several emails a day from people saying something along the lines of: 'Kate, I understand you've set up a network with X company. Could you possibly put our network in touch with their network?' Naturally, I felt honour-bound to realize these requests, since it met with the underlying philosophy of everything I was trying to do. However, it also tied me into lengthy email exchanges:

'George, I have just done some work with Jenny at X, and they are very interested in the network that you've set up at Y...'.

It was fantastic at one level, but it was also a lot of work that brought in no income, not to mention was taking up time when I could be doing the 'day job'. But the timing wasn't ideal. I had moved back into my parent's house in Feltham in 2010. It was supposed to be an interim measure after selling my tiny flat in Bermondsey. The goal was to find a larger three-bedroomed flat and I too needed an office to work from.

The plan didn't go as expected because, after selling my flat and spending the summer in Bahrain as I always did, I returned to the news that my Dad had bowel cancer. I ended up staying in Feltham for four years. Few people realized that while I was rushing around getting ERGs off the ground, I was living in Feltham, commuting back and forth into Central London as and when needed. The level of pain and exhaustion I endured was hard to manage. My hip had begun to wear loose once again, which made the journey unbearable at times. My mornings and evenings were now spent trying to be as supportive as possible to my parents, but it was hard to do anything too physical. Dad was in a lot of pain and Mum was distraught at the thought of losing him. We lived with a cloud of sadness about the inevitable end.

Nevertheless, the emails asking me to bring networks together kept rolling in. Everyone was asking the same thing, at the same time: 'Kate, you have to find a formal way to bring us all together. What are you going to do?'

I noticed that no one was asking what I *could* do any longer. It was what was I *going* to do? It was almost like it was my duty. It had turned into my responsibility to think about an elegant and cost-effective way to bring network leaders together and to ensure global relevance.

I went through various possible solutions in my mind and the clearest way forward seemed to be to build some sort of membership hub. It sounded good in theory, but I was also extremely reticent to lead something like this.

Aside from the difficulties of my then personal circumstance, the reason I had worked as a consultant was because I no longer wanted to head an institution. I like being creative and it can be hard to do that while leading an organization.

I procrastinated. I just didn't know the right thing to do. Eventually, a friend of mine took pity on me and began to prod me. She is a skilful coach who nudges you into answering the questions that sit in your head. As I listed the barriers and solutions, it started to sound a little simpler and more straightforward: build an online networking and professional development hub for disability employee resource group leaders, one which will also work as an essential resource for employers from all sectors and trades. In response, she reeled off a list of names who might be of use. There was this person who knew about databases, and this other expert who was good at building the type of platform I'd need.

'It's technology,' she pronounced. 'That's the only way to bring communities together around the world.'

She was completely right of course. I think I had always known that I would do it, but she really helped get it straight in my head. She helped me break down a big task into the next logical steps.

PurpleSpace experiment

I got started straight away, getting in touch with a lot of the people who were recommended and then others that subsequent friends and contacts pointed me towards.

I funded the initial work and people and tasks as well as the IT myself, but also managed to get some of the website and backend platform built at significantly less cost than it might have been.

Ever the one with a eye for marketing, I thought long and hard about what to call the new network of networks with the hundreds of thousands of employees with disability whose lives they would touch. In the end, there was only one obvious contender. I thought back to what I had floated earlier, the idea of promoting purple as an umbrella brand for employees with disability. It seemed perfect. A safe and informative 'purple space', for everyone to head to when they wanted to navigate the experience of ill health or disability, while still making progress at work. PurpleSpace it was.

Although the resulting PurpleSpace website looked quite flat on the front end, the back end was sophisticated, offering a wealth of useful resources for members to download, including all the publications, briefing papers and assets that I'd written over the previous years. It was designed to feel familiar and easy to use, operating a little like Facebook, so members could put up a profile and then form links with other members.

Amid setting up PurpleSpace, December 2014 through to March 2015 turned out to be a bleak moment in the lives of my family. Dad's cancer returned and it was terminal and he died quite soon after being admitted to a hospice.

The same week that Dad died my hip finally wore loose. We were all distraught about Dad's death and Mum the more so. I didn't know how to navigate the next period, now having to wait for surgery. For a long while, I existed in a complete fog that felt impossible to escape from. I had lost my dad, my mum was depressed, I was trying to set up PurpleSpace, but was still not 100 per cent sure I wanted to do it. Then, days before I was due to have my hip surgery, my mum fell over in the garden and broke her arm. It was hard not to laugh at the ludicrousness of the situation. I couldn't do anything with my lower limbs, while she couldn't do anything with her upper limbs. And then, the day before my surgery, my friend called. She had been diagnosed with breast cancer. That was the time when I truly thought I'd hit rock bottom. I had no energy left.

I did, of course, get through it and like millions before me it is simply those close loved ones, together with time and the company of good friends and work colleagues, that help you to gradually begin to put things back together. It didn't happen overnight, but things began to get a little bit better day by day, leading up to the launch of PurpleSpace on 15 October 2015. As so often happens, we weren't quite ready, but we launched anyway. We had a big event at the offices of the law firm Herbert Smith Freehills, with a turnout of more than 200 people. When it was my turn to take the platform, I spoke from the heart.

'This is an experiment,' I said. 'I have no idea if it will work but this is what you asked for.'

It was now up to the market to decide. And they did. Companies started to purchase their memberships straight away. Within the first year we managed to get enough in the kitty to take on our first member of staff to help me manage the growing service. In a classic Catch-22 situation though, I didn't have enough time to write the job description, or organize the process, because I was too busy being chief cook and bottle washer, doing absolutely everything. Fortunately, I happened to be in touch with Hays, the recruitment company and spoke with their Group Head of Equality, Diversity and Inclusion. They offered to help, but I had some quite strict criteria which were quite demanding,

I wanted someone who was good at admin, could engage our members, and was hardworking and fun to be with. Hays were amazing. They wrote up a full job description, shortlisted candidates and lined up five people for me to see. One of the five, was a standout candidate and, in April 2017 PurpleSpace had employee number one on board.

Now we were ready to see if this fledgling social business was able to achieve the big mission we'd been entrusted with. Was this the vehicle that would create a tipping point for disabled people in the workplace and truly make the difference I'd been working towards for years?

Then, three months after we were starting to get on top of things, I sent out my tweet: 'What about we start to light up purple on 3 December #IDPWD.'

A lesson to learn: the Purple Closet is a large space

There is no doubt that a lack of disabled 'role models' played a part in how I felt about myself in my early years of growing up. Not seeing people 'like you' can have a major impact on whether you chose to share information about your disability, or not. And even when you do first meet and interact with others with a disability, you may still be fighting demons about how you feel about being associated with 'outsiders'.

The first major study of what helps and what hinders the process of people sharing information about their disability at work was conducted in the research project that led to the messages in *Secrets & Big News*.[3] It was a detailed examination of the experiences of 2,511 employees with disabilities across 55 employer organizations. The research examined what makes it challenging to share personal information about disability, and what makes it easier.

Of the respondents who had not shared information about their disability with their employer, most respondents, at 60 per cent, said the main reason they did not do so is that they were worried that if they told their employer there may be repercussions either immediately or in the future.

The survey respondents repeatedly expressed views that suggested that for them the decision to identify with disability or ill health was an 'emotional' transaction. It required thought, reflection and anticipation about what might consequently follow.

Practical actions for employers and employees

For employers

RECOGNIZE THE REALITY
If you have conducted monitoring exercises and have secured data that suggests you have a lot fewer employees

with disability than reputable sources suggest you should have then don't go kidding yourself that your organization is 'different' and therefore less attractive to employees with disabilities. It is easy to fall into low-level thinking that your organization faces unique barriers to do with your 'sector' or 'trade' or size of your organization. I have heard it all in my career. It is very simple. You will already be employing people who have chosen not to 'come out'. The more you can build their trust, the more likely it is they will share their positive (or indeed, less than positive) experiences. And the more they share those positive experiences publicly then the more likely it is you will be able to attract candidates that may be a little further away from the jobs market. And the best way to build trust is to create an easy-to-use, visible workplace adjustment/accommodation process that is centralized and has internal service level agreements – one that your people can access in as dignified a way as possible.

RECTIFY THE NAMES

Many employers in their quest to remove reference to the word 'disability' (which is often seen as a pejorative expression) get too clever with the word 'disability'.

I have come across many organizations that strive too hard to remove the 'dis' from the word, straining themselves to get away from a word that has been poured over, debated and fought for decades. They disguise it, dress it down in lower case letters and stress ABILTY in upper case. Apart from those who have been very close to the history of the disability movement it is rare to find individuals in the employers' community who understand the importance of retaining words that, for all their challenges, mean something important.

I wrote in *Secrets & Big News* that the quotation from the 1602 play *Hamlet* by William Shakespeare – 'the lady doth protest too much, methinks' – often comes to mind when I see employers or indeed ERG leaders put ABILITY in capital letters when branding their networks.[4] The Shakespeare quote is used as a figure of speech to indicate that a person's overly frequent or vehement attempts to convince others of something often, ironically, help convince others that the opposite is true, by making the person look insincere or defensive.

My point here is not that it's a bad thing. It's a human thing and quite common.

However, try using the colour purple as a standout brand. Gillian Stamp of BIOSS, a global consultancy that enables organizations and leaders to understand human capability to realize their potential, reminded us just after the launch of PurpleSpace:

In the *Analects of Confucius* translation and notes by Simon Leys we are told that one day a disciple asked Confucius: 'If a king were to entrust you with a territory which you could govern according to your ideas, what would you do first?'

Confucius replied: 'My first task would certainly be to rectify the names.' On hearing this, the disciple was puzzled 'Rectify the names? And that would be your first priority? Is this a joke?'

Confucius explained: 'If the names are not correct, if they do not match realities, language has no object. If language is without an object, action becomes impossible

– and therefore, all human affairs disintegrate, and their management becomes pointless and impossible. Hence the very first task of a true statesman is to rectify the names.'

For employees

DON'T REINFORCE LOW EXPECTATIONS

Being our best at work might sometimes cause others to think that we are a bit of an inspiration. Some people who have impairments that are visible or that profoundly challenge peoples' views of human difference might be exposed to colleagues who think they are brave for simply getting up in the morning. Being the recipient of other peoples' inspiration is not our problem. Try not to internalize the reaction of others who sometimes call us brave, courageous or inspirational.

Simon Minty, stand-up comedian, disability consultant as well as Gogglebox superstar, calls out this phenomenon:

> Having a disability and being told you are inspirational can be flattering. When you've not actually done anything exceptional; going to work, going shopping, eating a meal it can become patronizing… I'm not keen on being called inspirational but I do like it if someone becomes 'inspired to do' something. So next time you are called inspirational for doing something mundane, ask the person what they're inspired to do, what changes and improvements will they now make as a result of meeting you?[5]

GET OVER THE CHAIR ENVY

When or if our employers get it right when it comes to delivering a seamless and easy-to-use workplace adjustment/accommodation process, they sometimes get a little influx of requests from people who 'want' adjustments/accommodations rather than 'need' them. We call this 'chair envy' when, for example, a request from someone who has developed a lower-back condition and needs an ergonomic chair to ensure the pain is at bay as they work for long periods at their desk triggers a wave of requests from others who would like a similar 'fancy' chair.

This is a tricky one. Work is hard. Everyone deserves the kit they need to get by. It's a human thing to want to make our lives a little easier. However, individuals who receive workplace adjustment/accommodations sometimes have to work with colleagues who want to know all about our whizz-bang kit and gizmos – in case they can get a slice of the pie. In order to survive, flourish and feel worthy it can be a good idea to have a one-liner ready to explain the reason without having to apologize or belittle your experience. If in doubt, get the mirror out and give yourself a top-up 'I am worth it' lesson.

CHAPTER THIRTEEN

Building disability confidence from the inside out

Building community and unity around purpose

Within seconds of sending out my tweet proposing to light up the world in purple on 3 December 2017 the likes and retweets came in. One of the first came from Penny Mordaunt, the then Minister of State for Disabilities in Theresa May's government. After that, the idea seemed to snowball, getting more and more attention. The feedback was unanimous, saying: yes, this is the next, most logical step. There was, however, also a very clear subtext: *Kate, you need to coordinate this.*

I barely had time to think *what have I done*, before I was inundated with expressions of interest from people who wanted to get involved. Most of the contacts came from PurpleSpace membership, but others seemed to find their way to my door, or email inbox, anyhow. My main message was that it was very much up to organizations to best decide what they did to signal their support. If everyone somehow stuck to the main point which was to celebrate the economic contribution of employees with a disability during the United Nations' International Day of Persons with Disabilities, then it felt logical for employees and employers to leverage the movement in a way that worked for them. Many ERG leaders decided to hold individual events, whether it was a keynote conference, or a coffee morning, or a seminar – all with a purple theme. Some senior executives saw it as an opportunity to look back and celebrate what their disability ERGs/networks had achieved in the past year, or to announce their plans for the following year. Some CEOs used it as an opportunity to get disability on their board agenda for the first time. Other businesses opted to become strategic allies and offered company-wide expressions of support for the day. They might bulk-order purple T-shirts or lanyards for their entire team. Others decided to swap their Twitter handle for a purple one, while some businesses planned to change their online logo for the day. The important thread was that employees with disabilities via ERGs were leading the march.

PurpleSpace did its best to try to keep a handle on co-ordination. We convened an official reference group of individuals drawn from our membership base who wanted to support what we were now calling #PurpleLightUp. They became a useful resource of advice and assistance to anyone wanting to get involved.

The day, 3 December, seemed to come around very quickly, and I was very curious to see what would actually happen. I tried to subdue that nervous feeling people often get before a big party. *Is anyone going to actually turn up?*

It turned out that I needn't have worried. When I got up in the morning, #PurpleLightUp was in third position on the list of trending items on Twitter. Ahead of us were Donald Trump who had said something characteristically outrageous overnight, and Prince Harry and Meghan who had announced their engagement a few days earlier. Twitter was alive with comments about #PurpleLightUp. I could hardly believe it.

Vanessa Hardy, our senior digital communications consultant, had been with me from the start of our journey. She is the skilful mastermind behind much of our work. She had joined me in my home-office in the build-up and together we both scrolled through Twitter, amazed at the sheer scale of the response. We had completely lost control of it, although in a good way. The grand Georgian façade of the headquarters of the Institute of Directors in London's Pall Mall had turned purple. Someone tweeted from the HQ of the Metropolitan Police on Victoria Embankment, showing that their building had had a similar purple treatment. Liverpool University was next. As we scrolled through Twitter, more and more initiatives were emerging by the second. Vanessa and I laughed as we complained almost simultaneously that our fingers ached as we tried to frantically keep up by liking and retweeting #PurpleLightUp, adding supportive messages.

As the exhausting but exhilarating day ended, we could draw only one conclusion: #PurpleLightUp had been a monumental success and I tried to define how I felt about it all. If I was honest, I was a little surprised by the scale of the response. I had never anticipated the sort of reaction it was getting. I was proud though. I had made it happen.

I had brought people together from around the around the world to *celebrate* disabled talent. That was cool. Throughout it all it had become clear that employees with disability wanted to lead and be seen to lead the process of cultural change. No more would they wait for chief executives to get interested. Neither would they tolerate 'waiting' for disability to get to the top of the list of diversity priorities. They felt part of a community of change makers.

Disability ERGs/networks: no longer a 'nice to have'

PurpleSpace received many approaches for membership in the months that followed. Leaders of disability ERGs/networks reported back that they now firmly had the attention of their chief executives following #PurpleLightUp. In turn, this meant that they had the opportunity to do things they'd been trying to get off the ground for years. Budgets were being scrutinized and raised, almost overnight.

A constant drip feed of negative stories can have an adverse effect

Why had it been such a success? I firmly believe it was all down to the celebratory theme. Over the years I have seen too many movements get stuck in a pattern of telling endless bad news stories and this doesn't force change. Indeed, a constant drip feed of negative stories, and long lists of things that still need to be done, can have an adverse effect. Most of us are well-meaning, but it's hard not to resent being constantly battered over the head, being told: do more! For decades, much about disability had been a bad news story. I had long since decided that this was the wrong way to approach things. Many of the communities we were talking about and to were really struggling with this human experience. Individuals were unhappy, depressed even, about how tough life can sometimes be. The hard-hitting campaigns were adding to those feelings of despair. We also had to accept that among those who had no experiences of disability there was often an attitude that what they did was not discrimination. If they thought about it deeply at all, they would say that disability is just something that happens to others. It is unfortunate, but the world is just not designed for everyone.

Over the years, businesses had been seeing the exact same statistics I'd been exposed to, over and over. 'One in two disabled people are out of work.' If you are a recruiter at a large firm, how does this statistic incentivize you to give a position to the unemployed second person with a disability? Let's turn it round. Wouldn't it be far better if the statistics highlighted the wonderful contribution being made by the 'one out of two' who *is* in employment? How have they made their mark on the fortunes of their departments? What difference did bringing in this talent make? We needed to talk more about who is brilliant out there.

A *Forbes* article in 2022 describes Scott-Parker's take on the more traditional approach of focusing on 'numbers' to drive change. It doesn't work. As she says:

> Campaigners fail when they try to challenge the emotional factors that get in the way with 'logic' – as though somehow statistics (ie 1.3 billion people with disabilities) will change behaviours, when these same behaviours may be justified,

but not driven by, apparent logic and when change is often not in the gift of the person reading the campaign. Face-to-face contact is essential, ie people with disabilities and people in business having contact informally/formally, learning from and with each other, be it structured consultations, lunches, internships, business leader to leader with disabilities conversations, disabled employee networks, #PurpleLightUp celebrations, award ceremonies and more.[1]

I suspected that this age-old tendency towards the negative was at the heart of the reason that the United Nation's annual International Day of Persons with Disabilities (IDPD) event had never quite galvanized action when it came to the employment prospects of employees with disabilities. It always had a theme, an important theme, whether it was about poverty, or famine, or folk not being able to access good healthcare or hygiene. While each of these subjects are incredibly important and it is 100 per cent right to draw attention to them, they are not the whole story of disability and of course many employers are not mandated to 'campaign' for change for employees with a disability. So, there was no unifying force for the employers' community when it came to IDPD.

Now we'd found the sweet spot, the buzz that united everyone around a movement, everyone was keen to maintain the momentum. The one thing that I heard again and again was: What are we going to do next year? I was committed.

It took a few weeks for things to calm down. I was punch drunk after weeks of living with a heady combination of exhaustion, over-excitement and non-stop juggling.

I found it very difficult to fight off the deep feelings of responsibility that washed over me. My good friends rallied around, laughing when I reverted to the familiar refrain: I just want to gift wrap PurpleSpace and #PurpleLightUp and give it all away. Of course, I didn't mean it, but I needed to create a better more sustainable plan.

True to type I managed to consider fresh steps by looking on the positive side of what we'd managed to achieve. My work with PurpleSpace has been all about finding a way to help disabled talent bolster itself, build confidence and boost self-esteem. I know that feeling of being demoralized and have heard so many heart-breaking stories of people feeling down on themselves. That feeling can last a lifetime. However, we all have a role to play in this. Disabled people have skin in the game. It's not always about other people and systems and barriers. It's about us. #PurpleLightUp united us all, employers and employees.

I recall most the many personal stories I was told by people who were thrilled by #PurpleLightUp. One that touched me the most was a note I received from a single mum in Sheffield, whose young son had cerebral palsy. She wrote: 'This just gives me hope.'

This wasn't a story about deficit, or pity, or shame; it was a celebration

She was right too. Underlying all the messages was an electrifying feeling of positivity. This wasn't a story about deficit, or pity, or shame; it was a celebration. People were feeling good about being part of this movement. The world that this young boy from Sheffield would grow up in would be a very different place than the one that confronted me, as a

15 year old who was unexpectedly diagnosed with juvenile chronic arthritis. This mother can now hope that her son will one day have a job. And all being well, the fact that it will be so much more than a 'little job' won't even be a matter for discussion.

Supporting those with skin in the game to work to purpose

There are many ways the world changes. Sometimes, it changes because something cataclysmic happens and people feel forced to stand up and call out terrible atrocities, or subrogation of individuals, by saying: not in my name. We very much saw this in 2020, with the explosion of support for the Black Lives Matter movement, following the brutal murder of George Floyd in Minneapolis. The other big pivotal point is where the world celebrates the talent, or potential, inherent in all its citizens. It is a message born out of hope for a better world. Both shifts in the way we think drive systemic change in human rights and justice. For us, the firm choice for #PurpleLightUp was to continue the celebratory theme but just to make it even bigger.

Together with PurpleSpace members, we came to the firm conclusion that it was much stronger to continue to deliver positive messages saying: *recruit and celebrate purple talent!* Be part of this celebration. On #PurpleLightUp we needed to be out there, loudly shouting about the amazingly talented people in our midst and the fantastic economic contribution they achieved. That was what 3 December needed to be about. To join, business leaders would be forced to think: What have we really done? Can we authentically be part of this event? This is what triggers change.

For a brief while, I had some concerns that #PurpleLightUp might be seen to be too frivolous, if there was too much glamour, glitz and fun. Would people think it was it all fur coat and no knickers, as they say? I also really did have to pause to think deeply whether it was right for PurpleSpace to become too closely associated with this idea. I concluded it was right to have that link. #PurpleLightUp was life-affirming, when so much in the narrative of disabled people is negative. It is a broad story that celebrates the economic contribution of employees with a disability. The movement would also give us the opportunity to spread the message wider and globally.

#PurpleLightUp celebrates the economic contribution of employees with a disability

In Year Two of #PurpleLightUp we were approached by Channel 4, who were keen to get involved. The channel has long been known for championing diversity and was keen to build on the success of *The Last Leg*, a late-night show that had premiered during the 2012 Paralympics and grown into a popular series. The bare bones of the idea that they came to me with was that the presenter Adam Hills would front a short film showcasing the real stories from people with disabilities from our membership and the result could be aired on the day of the next event as an extended advert.

Cost was obviously a factor, since things like this don't come cheap. Channel 4 said they'd cover the cost of the filming and crew, but PurpleSpace would need to help them find the broadcast fees.

'Would any of your members be willing to contribute?' I was asked.

This was the cue for me to play cupid between Channel 4 and a good number of our members. I suspected they would come up trumps and sure enough, eight of them did, including BT, HSBC, Lloyds of London, Virgin Media and Nationwide.

Discussions went on for weeks and weeks, but we never really seemed to get to the point where the TV producers gave us a 100 per cent commitment. Meanwhile, all I could do was to get stuck in to planning the rest of the event, not to mention juggling the needs of the day job at PurpleSpace.

There were positive signs that other campaigners were beginning to do some fantastic and innovative things to promote disabled talent. Caroline Cassey, the wonderfully sassy, outgoing activist and campaigner, whom I had known for some years, was due to launch Valuable 500 in 2019. This was her innovative campaign to gather 500 multinational corporations to work together to unlock the business, social and economic value of people living with disability. The idea of the campaign was to push for a structure of accountability among corporate leaders and ensure they recognized the inherent value of the talent in employees with a disability. To do this, they needed to put disability on the board agenda. What I most liked about Valuable 500 was that the new movement would make it easier for CEOs to lean into what needed to be done. It was a no-brainer that PurpleSpace would fully support Valuable 500 and has been proud to do so ever since its launch at Davos.

Eight weeks before the second #PurpleLightUp, Channel 4 finally gave the much-anticipated promotional film the green light. They produced a powerful two-minute film featuring employees drawn from all the sponsors. After an opening sequence where individuals voiced the dismissive terms so many people have used when describing employees with a disability, such as they are a 'token hire' or a 'drain on resources', the film turns those perceptions on their head. Through individual, uplifting stories, the stars of the ad show speak about what a difference they have made. It focused on our core messages: that the celebration of the economic contribution of employees with disabilities was, until then, an untold story.

The film first aired after *The Last Leg* on 30 November, and then was repeated throughout the weekend. It was odd seeing the #PurpleLightUp logo prominently displayed on the small screen, but very exciting too.

The actual day of the 2018 #PurpleLightUp followed a very similar pattern to the first, except the event was bigger than ever. I knew for a fact that this movement had the potential to be a global and enduring force for change.

One of the disability ERG leaders from one of our member companies called me. I had helped her to set up their disability network.

'This is us now, leading this movement, you know that?' she said.

'Yes,' I replied.

'You can let go,' she went on.

'I know,' I replied.

'I have only got 10 minutes before I board a flight to Seattle,' she went on. 'My phone is about to die. I must finish up a big law case for my team. There is a lot riding on it. Wish I could join you, but the day job is calling. I don't fancy getting my butt kicked. I wanted you to know I just spent £500 on a pair of purple designer earrings because I can. I think I need to start identifying with the experience of disability. I just wanted you to know we've got this. It's up to us now. Not you.'

'Yes,' I replied.

'It is down to us to lead,' she said as the phone died.

Building inner confidence

On a personal level, what pleased me most was that the #PurpleLightUp movement had become so closely aligned with inner disability confidence. Yes, we had huge numbers of companies that wanted to be involved and which were looking to support #PurpleLightUp. It was a sign that they either had disability on the board agenda or wanted to celebrate the fact they had an employee resource group, or that they saw themselves as an ally.

Employees the world over were saying: we are leading

What brought it all together though was the passion of employees with a disability who wanted to be heard. They were driving this now. Employees the world over were saying: we are leading. My tax goes into the economy of my home country, and I am doing my best.

We were changing the narrative.

The language around disability was no longer about deficit, or 'lack of' or sadness. It was about getting on with it. Telling our story and supporting our employers. In turn, we were supporting those who come behind us.

While there was an incredible opportunity to spread the message like nothing I had ever known, I still needed to solve the problem of how to build on the success of the event. If we wanted to expand PurpleSpace I would need more help, I would need a more resilient infrastructure. Membership fees were not enough to cover the costs of the team I'd need to recruit to really build the movement. Where did I go from here?

A lesson to learn: assume you know nothing

Assumptions, when it comes to people with lived experience of disability and ill health, are largely unhelpful.

Knowing one person with a visual impairment is to know one person with a visual impairment. It doesn't mean that you know the myriad of experiences that people have, nor even the summation of barriers that might exist or the best access adjustments/accommodations that might help other people with a visual impairment.

There is one experience that I frequently encounter that tests my personal level of patience. It's the common human tendency to compare someone's lived experience of disability with that of another. If I had one British pound for each time I have stepped into a taxi in many cities across the world to end up in conversation with a taxi driver's very long story about their own mother's hip replacement, I would be a very rich woman. It has taught me much about the human psychology of the non-disabled person's experience of disability and ill health. Mostly that, at best, it is largely irrelevant and, at its worse, a distraction as others try to grapple with information and experiences that they do not understand.

I am often reminded, in such situations, of the phrase 'I'm not racist, I have black friends' or the variation 'Some of my best friends are black'. It is an argument which is often used by white people to justify their claim that they are not racist towards black people. A 2004 study in *Basic and Applied Social Psychology* list the phrase as a 'common [claim of] innocence by association'.[2] In 2011 a study was published in the *Journal of Black Studies* entitled 'African Americans' lay theories about the detection of prejudice and non-prejudice', in which it was suggested that African Americans were rarely impressed by whites claiming to have 'black friends', and that the claim was more likely to make African Americans think that the person making it was in fact more, not less, prejudiced.[3] The phrase is cited as an instance of 'resistance to antiracist thinking'. There are many calls to dismantle the logic of the phrase. For some it is akin to the ludicrous suggestion there is no such thing as sexism because we all have a close friend or family member who is a woman.[4]

One day in a 'mid-flight' rant about the phenomenon that many disabled people experience when total strangers feel able to share intimate details about the lives of others who are supposedly their friends and loved ones, I was challenged by a trusted colleague working at C-suite level. 'Is your irritation more or less than that which you have for incompetent diversity and inclusion professionals?' he asked with a wry smile. 'Less,' I had to admit. 'Is your irritation more or less than that you have for inept politicians?' he asked, still smiling. 'A lot less,' I said now quite enjoying the challenge.

'Might it be that all human beings are trying to understand the lives of others by looking through the lenses of those closest to us?' he concluded.

Of course, he is right. But this knowledge does nothing to stop the prickle every time a new acquaintance tells me about their painful knee or the fact their dog or best friend now has arthritis. It isn't so much that I don't care about peoples' knees or dogs or the friends of others. It's more a case that the journey is hard and hearing others simply 'name-check' someone else in their life makes me want to punch them on the nose. And of course, I have never experienced the statement 'I'm not disablist, my best friend has arthritis.' Though that is probably more to do with the fact that many people do not immediately perceive the challenge of disability as a societal one that can cause discrimination. It is often still seen as a medical one, and an unlucky one that will make life a lot less enjoyable at that.

It is always safe to assume you know nothing when hearing the stories of others. You start from ground zero.

Practical actions for employers and employees

For employers

USE SOCIAL MEDIA INFLUENCERS

The use of social media, as a force for good, has been a game-changer for many people with disabilities. Consider how your organization could use one of the many incredible disabled social media influencers to nudge your thinking in building your brand as one known to learn directly from people with disabilities. Check out the Purple Goat Agency, the specialist social and influencer disability marketing agency, if you need convincing of the value of doing so.[5]

MANDATE NEW LEADERS

Reflect on that hurried call I got from a highly respected lawyer just off to Seattle. She is most known for her work to reduce the gender pay gap. She is expected to become a partner of a global law firm within the next couple of years. She has just 'come out' as neuro-divergent to her immediate colleagues and plans to tell 5,000 of her colleagues at the next town hall. The individuals leaning in and leading change are priceless. Notice who they are and give them a mandate.

For employees

SHARE YOUR STORY

Think about the benefit and long-term value of you sharing your story of a successful workplace adjustment/

accommodation process either within your organization or externally. None of us want to be held up as 'inspiration porn' but if our stories help just one more person down the road, it might be worth it.

NETWORK WITH FELLOW TRAVELLERS

Never, ever underestimate the value of talking to and networking with the many other fellow travellers who experience disability at work, and often in our own workplaces. Get involved in your organizations' ERG/network. And get over yourself if you think that by doing so it will damage your credibility, your image, your promotion prospects. We are not the only folk who have fallen into the habit of hiding or masking our experiences. John Browne, the former chief executive at BP, describes in *The Glass Closet* his experiences as a closeted gay man in the oil industry and the experiences of other gay and lesbian leaders from around the world. He argues that coming out is best for employees and the companies that support them.

He says:

> I wish I had been brave enough to come out earlier during my tenure as chief executive of BP. I regret it to this day. I know that if I had done so I would have made more of an impact for other gay men and women. It is my hope that the stories in this book will give some of them the courage to make an impact of their own.[6]

CHAPTER FOURTEEN

The futurists

Go big or go home

Christmas 2018 and I met up with my mentor, Susan Scott-Parker. Straight away she asked me what was happening with PurpleSpace and #PurpleLightUp.

'You need a bigger team around you,' she said. 'Time to think about your next stage of development.'

She was right, I knew that. I'd worked out that we needed seed funding of around £300,000 to employ three or four more staff to really build the movement.

Another conversation with a mentor reminded me of our senior allies. 'You've created something incredible though the time is right to ask corporates to step up and invest in this employee movement.'

I thought back to a conversation I'd had a few years before with Gavin Bounds, the then Chief Operating Officer for Fujitsu. He'd been supportive of PurpleSpace from the off, not just by signing up as one of our members, but also in a personal way. About one year after the launch of PurpleSpace, he had said something which I had squirrelled away in the back of my mind for a later date.

'This isn't for now, but one day, Kate, you will come to me with a bigger ask,' he had said.

The clear implication was that he would be open to that bigger ask when it eventually came.

I realized that the moment for the Big Ask had now arrived.

Our conversations, when they happened, couldn't have gone better. Gavin agreed to the request for £30,000 towards investing in more people; he also said he'd help in any other way he could. This was great. I became emboldened to seek other corporate sponsors.

I also wanted Gavin to host a dinner for (other) chief executives and senior executives, which would send the message, 'This is what Fujitsu is doing, and we think you should do that too.'

I wanted the dinner to look and smell completely different to fundraising. Other corporates were far more likely to respond positively if they saw a big firm like Fujitsu throwing its weight behind PurpleSpace and the #PurpleLightUp movement. Gavin said he would need to speak with Fujitsu's chief executive about hosting a dinner and then come back to me. He did, however, seem quite supportive of the idea.

Inviting senior champions to follow, not lead

It was agreed. Fujitsu would become #PurpleLightUp's first strategic founding partner. Duncan Tait, the then CEO of Fujitsu, would host the corporate dinner to help attract other sponsors and Gavin would become PurpleSpace's chair.

The dinner when it occurred was a lavish affair at which Duncan Tait spoke. He grabbed everyone's attention. After opening with amusing anecdotes and getting the room laughing, he started to talk about the gender pay gap, which was very much in the news at that time as the strong campaign gained ground. As a father of four daughters, he said it was his duty to actively pursue policies that would see an end to this unfair practice.

He neatly segued the conversation to disability.

'Many of the people in this room will acquire a disability before we retire. I am not sure how many people are aware of this, but 83 per cent of all the people with disabilities in the world, acquire their disability during the course of their working life.'

The speech opened the way for us to talk to all those who were now ready to listen. I didn't waste the opportunity and that event paved the way for me to hold proper talks in the weeks and months to come, to ensure that #PurpleLightUp was a serious contender when annual budgets were set. If ever there was a tipping point for the #PurpleLightUp movement, this was it. Over the following months we signed up support from Project People, Scope, Enterprise Rent-A-Car and ABM. HSBC and Anglo American were added to the list. Sometime later Salesforce joined. This funding meant we would be able to start employing a team from late 2019 which would ensure that the fourth annual celebration in 2020 would be the biggest, best and most organized one yet.

Collaboration is the only way in crowded markets

Of course, #PurpleLightUp 3 was looming.

With the support of allies at Virgin Media we found a taxi company to wrap a cab in purple free of charge. Over the following two weeks I persuaded key business leaders to agree to be 'kidnapped' and bundled into a purple taxi to be interviewed. It was a huge amount of fun on the day too. It was a thrown-together, impulsive event, but that was part of the beauty of it. We videoed all of the interviews from our kidnappees. A wonderful independent film-maker George Bounds from Wippasnappa created the most exciting films and edited them magnificently. At the end of the film you can see us laughing outside Marks & Spencer on Oxford Street. Exhausted, joyous, amazed at how the world was lighting up purple as a mark of respect to those employees with disabilities in work around the world.

That year the movement became international and in quite a dramatic way too. Niagara Falls turned purple, as did the parliament building in Vienna and we heard numerous reports of individuals all over the world supporting us through their own physical and online events, and workplace initiatives. Plus, once again, we trended on Twitter. This time in the top position.

It takes a global pandemic to make remote working possible

Our new recruits joined us between February and March 2020. Then, of course, Covid-19 arrived and our plans, like everyone else's were thrown into chaos. I had three brand new staff members at almost the exact moment the country went into total lockdown. It was not the ideal circumstance, not by a long way.

I briefly considered furloughing everyone and trying again whenever I could, but it wasn't possible. We had the momentum, and we couldn't stop. Disability ERGs were increasingly seen as the drivers for cultural change. Non-disabled privilege still existed; indeed, it had been there all along. Now, though, numerous voices had got together to demand change. There is power in numbers.

Disability ERGs were increasingly seen as the drivers for cultural change

There was another important reason why we needed to keep on pressing forward too. With Covid-19 it was increasingly important for disability ERGs to advise their organizations on the best way to create remote working policies. For years they had been advocating the need for flexible working as one way of delivering workplace adjustments. It felt as if overnight, in the most challenging and dramatic of circumstances, the world, it seemed, was now working remotely in a super-charged digital era. One day that would change, but for now we had to help many people notice that the 'privilege' now being offered to us all would be something we would want to preserve and protect for a long time hence.

The coronavirus pandemic accelerated digital progress by three years, according to a report by the Centre for Economic and Business Research (CEBR) for Virgin Media 02 Business. The impact of this is already apparent, with more businesses than ever allowing employees to work from home on a full-time or flexible basis.

With so many workers having continued their jobs from their own homes throughout the pandemic, it's clear that the world is ready to adjust to a lifestyle where people no longer need to be in an office from 9 to 5. The report showed that just under four million people who were previously 'locked out' of employment (including 1.5 million disabled people, 1.2 million parents and 500,000 carers) would be more inclined to take a job that offers remote working.[1]

The world is ready to adjust to a lifestyle where people no longer need to be in an office from 9 to 5

We kept going.

The plan for #PurpleLightUp 2020 was a 24-hour global broadcast filled with webinars, interviews and panel discussions. It was going to be a lot of work and certainly harder than jumping into a taxi and kidnapping eight executives. It meant we needed to get speakers from around the world and it was a big digital logistical exercise. The team worked brilliantly together in order to deliver. We called on a lot of the international contacts I had made over the years who opened up their contact books and helped me to persuade people from the four corners of the world to participate. Despite the challenges of the pandemic, the 2020 #PurpleLightUp movement added partners in the Middle East, the United States, India and Australia. Among our new international partners, we secured a rich combination of representatives from employers' organizations and trade associations as well as global multinationals. We were asking a lot from our partners, to fill four-hour slots with speakers, but they rose to the challenge.

In 2020 the support of the International Labour Organization (ILO), a United Nations agency with a mandate to advance social and economic justice, was remarkable. Most importantly, the ILO is the organization that is most associated with the theme of each International Day of Persons with Disabilities (IDPD). We'd been working with Stefan Trömel, its senior disability specialist, for a while. I'd got to know him after he'd invited me to speak at ILO's 2019 conference in Geneva and we'd spoken on and off since then. I was, clearly, keen to get some sort of support or recognition from the ILO for #PurpleLightUp. I was keen to ensure #PurpleLightUp did not distract from the intent behind International Day of Persons with Disabilities, which had become a national fixture since 1992. I didn't want to take anything away from the IDPD, with its own aims, which were: to promote an understanding of disability issues and mobilize support for the dignity, rights and well-being of persons with disabilities.

It took a bit of courage to broach the subject but when I did, I was impressed by Stefan's enthusiasm.

Our connection with the International Labour Organization opened another, unexpected, but large and highly influential door for #PurpleLightUp: Netflix. The streaming giant had produced a documentary called *Crip Camp*, with support from Michelle and Barack Obama, and they were keen to get extensive exposure. Stefan suggested a connection during #PurpleLightUp might be an opportune way of highlighting the birth of the disability rights movement.

Crip Camp is a documentary which begins at a US summer camp in the early 1970s. Camp Jened was not far from the site of the legendary Woodstock festival, but what made it different was that it was for disabled teens, a rare utopia in a far less tolerant world. For the first time in their lives, these teenagers were not judged from an abled-bodied perspective. What made it really interesting, though, was that the camp's radical vision went on to shape decades of disabled activism. The documentary maker, Jim Le Brecht, an award-winning sound designer, who also has spina bifida and uses a wheelchair, had kickstarted the film project after becoming convinced that the others who were at that camp with him had come together to make change. Sure enough, he found others who had been inspired by the experience, such as Judy Heumann, a polio survivor and disability rights crusader, who served as a special advisor to Barack Obama. It is a fascinating documentary, designed to reframe how people thought about disability. How could I not want to be involved? After discussions with Netflix and ILO, we hashed out a plan for them to have a slot for *Crip Camp* in our 24-hour global broadcast.

We started the global broadcast at 10pm, GMT, on 2 December 2020, kicking off in Oceania and then chased the sun across the world into, and then throughout, 3 December. Each continent provided up to five hours of broadcast content. Some of the material was pre-recorded with panels made up of some incredible senior leaders, but some of the programming was live. It was all a bit of a juggle, but then it wouldn't be a #PurpleLightUp without a bit of chaos. We were also careful not to lose the sense of fun and celebration that had made the previous #PurpleLightUps so special, and the 2020 event was billed as a 24-hour party with a purpose.

Even before the broadcast began, it was clear we had a very big party indeed on our hands. From Monday 30 November, my Twitter feed was full of dramatic purple pictures and messages of support. This time, as well as UK landmarks being lit up from the Blackpool Tower to the London Eye, there were iconic buildings, from around the world, bathed in purple. Everything from the FC Bayern Munich Allianz Arena to the control tower at John F Kennedy airport in New York, to Sydney Harbour Bridge were loud and proud in purple, signalling their support in celebrating the economic contribution of the 386 million employees with disability of working age around the world. When it came to the UK broadcast, we opened with the news that then-Prime Minister Boris Johnson had tweeted in support:

> On #IDWPWD, I pay tribute to the extraordinary contribution people living with disabilities make to this country.
>
> Next year we will publish the most ambitious disability plan in a generation – so there are no barriers to anyone reaching their full potential. #PurpleLightUp.

To drive the message home, Boris Johnson wore a purple tie in the House of Commons that day.

The day itself was exhausting as ever, but also just as much fun. Even though some of the sessions were pre-recorded, we didn't get much rest. When I wasn't on screen,

I was sitting on my sofa mainlining coffee while glued to the Twitter feed, or watching the comments section of the broadcast as people logged in and chatted about what was being said on screen.

Businesses that had never before been engaged in the campaign, and indeed with which I had never, were now stepping up and celebrating. The facilities team at New York's Freedom Tower all wore purple and arranged for the iconic tower to be lit up in purple. It felt like the world had become smaller through so many people thinking about and honouring others who live with a human experience they'd really rather not live with. The business leaders who appeared on the broadcast were amazing. As they talked, I was quite taken with how confident they spoke, as allies. This was no longer something they were all feeling their way around, desperate not to do or say the wrong thing. Disability and celebrating disabled talent were now unequivocally on the agenda. It wasn't about 'doing good' or philanthropy. Disability ERGs are, as Ian Stuart, the CEO of HSBC UK, said, a 'critical business influencer' and have to be part of boardroom thinking. They are here to stay.

Disability and celebrating disabled talent were now unequivocally on the agenda

Who would have thought that a single colour could so effectively bring together the world and capture the imagination in such a powerful way? The entire had been just so positive and life-affirming. That day, 3 December 2020, was absolutely the day that we united as a 386-million-strong international community, with the full support of many millions more. Going forward, there really is no limit to what we can now achieve together.

The future is here: the third phase of change

Today, the future has arrived. At PurpleSpace we have a term for those remarkable organizations who invest in the process of learning directly from their own people via the investment of their disability ERGs. We call it the third phase of change.

The first phase was about legislation. It was about understanding and embedding the disability-specific equalities legislation first developed in countries such as the United States and the UK, and now, through the UN Convention, across the world.

The second phase was about employers: the process by which they have become, and continue to become, disability-confident and disability-smart organizations with the assistance of best practice tools and enabling products. That phase of employer development continues and is often made easier by the extraordinary work of the national employer organizations such as BDF, AND, Disability:In or indeed international mobilization and innovation from GBDN and Valuable 500.

Meanwhile, the third phase has begun. It is about disabled employees creating a fresh conversation about how we get ahead at work, how we build personal resilience and how we can bring our authentic selves to work for personal and business benefit.

As we build our Networkology Academy and leadership know-how it will be interesting to watch the new breed of savvy disability ERG leaders claim their space.

At PurpleSpace, we often talk about the loneliness of the long-distance ERG leader. These are the people who have full-time day jobs over and above their ERG role. I find it enormously exciting to see how they 'take on' their organizations in a way that they want their employer to win. Sometimes they get bruised. Sometimes they get promoted. Sometimes they move on. But nearly always they are forever changed by leaning in, understanding the art and the science of leading change and making a difference.

When we run peer group sessions, I look around the faces in the virtual room and see the excitement. Someone from Lloyds Banking Group will be sitting next to a person from Clifford Chance, who is sitting next to a Merck employee, who is sitting next to a GSK one. Everybody's job is different but what they have is this common desire to build a better working world for employees with a disability. They look into each other's eyes or listen to each other's voices or read the captions our speech-to-text masters, MyClearText, and the loneliness dissipates. They all want their organizations to succeed and will push past inelegant experiences they have had. Or indeed illegal and damaging ones. They want to learn, pass it on, push on through.

Tapping into and supporting the energy, passion and commitment of these 'volunteers' has been a real honour. I enjoy how they build community and unity through #PurpleLightUp and indeed throughout their busy year. They continue to build disability confidence from the inside out. They share that with allies. They invite allies in.

They tweak their focus, fire up their people. And they go again.

A lesson to learn: assimilating disability as part of our identity takes a lifetime

An uninvited change of identity takes time to make sense of, to regroup on what life might look like, and to 'go again'. Everybody will have their own timeline in assimilating the experience. Some fast, some slow. Some have setbacks. Some will forever struggle. Employers will never know that level of detail and can never assume the time it takes for people who may be 'defined' as being disabled (in ways that might mean they are protected by legislation) to start identifying with the term and use it to define an aspect of themselves.

In 2019 Steve Ingham had already been CEO of the Page Group for 13 years and with the company since 1987. He had played a strong leadership role in helping the organization grow from a few hundred people to a FTSE 250 group that employs more than 6,500 people across 37 countries. While skiing in the Alps he had fallen off a narrow bridge into a gully, and had fractured his spine. Ingham:

> recounts the accident in the short, matter of fact sentences
> of a tale often told – but still has to stop for a few seconds
> to compose himself when describing the worry imposed on
> his family through the period. It is the only time that Ingham
> shows the emotional toll alongside the physical injury that
> left him facing a battle simply to get out of bed.[2]

Practical actions for employers and employees

For employers

CONSIDER BEING A FUTURIST

If you are not already, seriously consider being a futurist. Invest in your own home-grown freedom fighters for they want you to succeed. 'Investment' means different things for different organizations. For some it will mean formalizing the role of the ERG leader and allowing them a certain amount of 'facility time' in order that they can work on the activities of the network. For others it will be about enabling their fast-track access to high-end leadership training. For others in could mean monetary reward.

In 2021 LinkedIn announced it would pay employee resource group leaders a $10,000 monetary compensation for each year served. Preceding the LinkedIn announcement, Twitter also declared their commitments for additional ERG financial rewards. Justworks, an HR tech company, has an ERG leader compensation package that includes stock options and monetary reward.[3]

Whatever investment might mean, the point is that if you want to do more than play with the possibility of culture change you would be wise to invest in the future of disability confidence via the establishment of ERGs.

HELP BUILD INNER CONFIDENCE

Do not get fixated on skilling-up huge numbers of non-disabled colleagues to learn how to better connect with us, talk to us, have conversations with us. Whether that's about unconscious bias programmes or 'awareness' training.

These things are mostly superficial. Disability confidence is a two-way street – no point in investing in the skills of non-disabled colleagues without equally considering the need to help individuals build inner confidence to navigate the soft bigotry of low expectation. This land is ours too. Nothing without us.

For employees

IDENTIFY THE IMPORTANT CEOS

Talent-spot the CEOs that really matter in our lives. Seriously. Cultivate the habit of identifying and noticing the key messages they offer in their desire to build a better working world for employees with disabilities. Ian Stuart, CEO of HSBC UK, is open and generous in his desire to ensure people with disabilities at HSBC do well at work. In a podcast with Alia Cooper, who is Global Co-chair at HSBC Ability, he says, 'If you give a bit you get an awful lot back.'[4] He talks openly about why he is honest about his family experiences of disability – like my friend Karen all those years ago, he is unconcerned with the optics – he cares very little about the personal implications of putting yourself out in order to deliver well as an ally. He just does. And no, I am not saying, by any stretch of the imagination, that in our search for employment we must target those companies who have a CEO gifted enough to state their strategic ambitions in plain sight. On the contrary, we must believe deeply that the combination of our skills together with the impact of anti-discrimination legislation, and networking with others who have navigated the hard stuff, will offer the best shot we have in securing and retaining gainful employment. But while those employment gaps remain, we must, first and foremost, replenish ourselves with knowledge that there are business leaders who do 'get this stuff'.

DON'T BELIEVE THE 'NAYSAYERS'

Don't believe those who insist that the business community is not open to recruiting people with disabilities. This is not my experience. It is a million miles away from being true.

Afterword

A friend once joked with me about that saying that no one on their deathbed ever said they wished they'd spent more time at the office.

'You'll be the one saying: I wish I can have *just one more day* in the office,' she said.

She is wrong. Hybrid and remote working with accessible technology now means I can work anywhere. I'm kidding with you. The point she is trying to make is not lost on me and in writing this book, I can see a definite theme: I work hard. I have always worked hard. I have missed out on time with friends, family and loved ones. And during moments when I have worked all day and through the night, it has felt hard. Though I have enjoyed my career and it is I who has been the lucky one.

As I end this description of my positively purple road of discovery, I am reminded of five enduring life lessons which I would offer any reader. Whether you are a diversity and inclusion professional, a human resource professional, a CEO or a disability ERG leader. Or indeed a parent, a doctor or a journalist. Wherever you sit in your circle of influence, when it comes to building a better working world for people with disabilities, these lessons may help you. Driving culture change is a long road, made shorter when you practise the art of self-reflection and the ability to seek out wise council.

The first is that 'Obstinacity' is a helpful characteristic. See what you can do to cultivate it. It is in my blood and no transplant will ever remove it and there is little point in fighting it. It's a mash up of two words – a mixture of 'obstinance' (unyielding stubborn adherence to one's purpose or opinion) and 'tenacity' (the tendency to be very determined). I sometimes wish I was less 'obstinaceous', as it might have allowed me to work less and watch Netflix more, but there you go. I apologize to the thousands who have had to bear my impatient and unrelenting focus. Especially if I asked for things inelegantly or ever suggested anyone's personal contributions were not valuable. But only a little bit. I had to keep moving. If something is worth fighting for, then cultivate the art of being obstinaceous.

The second lesson has been to accept that you really can't get toothpaste back in the tube. It's a figure of speech to illustrate the irreversibility of an action. There isn't a day that goes by where I don't (at least partly) regret suggesting to the world on Twitter that the time had come to use the colour purple to bring disability ERGs/networks together to celebrate our economic contribution. Nurturing the movement has been a joy and a curse. But sometimes knowing there is no way back is liberating and, while I will shape and lead the movement a little longer, it is comforting to know there is no way back and others will lead. I see how it is enabling employees with disability, together with our allies and champions, an opportunity to be a central force in the next phase of the disability movement.

This lesson holds true for anyone who has ever pushed and pushed for something they believe in and when you undertake an action that cannot be retracted. While my example was high-stakes there are myriads of things we might say or do to try to change the world, or other people's views that may involve short-term pain. Sometimes we may even have to leave relationships or indeed our employers to stand up for what we believe in. So long as our intent is based on wanting to make things better, we must be prepared to make some waves and collect some enemies.

Thirdly, I have learnt that improving employer policy in relation to employing people with disability will only get us so far, whether that's achieved by skilful legislators, D&I professionals or committed CEOs who courageously and rightly put disability on the board agenda. The next period of systemic culture change will come from the millions of employees with disability who vocalize their experiences in building inner confidence and lead the change. So that we can learn from each other. Of this, I know. It will be our stories that change the world. The ones we tell ourselves and each other in order to decide how we project to others.

Again, this lesson is an important one for anyone wanting to do anything at scale when it comes to the life chances of disabled people. Invest less in helping non-disabled people to get better at working with us and much more in helping employees with disability to learn the skills that will enable us to secure what we need. The majority of us know what is reasonable.

My fourth life lesson is to ask the right questions. I suspect when it comes to building a better working world for employees with disability, we will see large-scale 'disinvestment' of training programmes for non-disabled colleagues about the ins and outs of how to work with the likes of me. Instead, we will see it reinvested in the confidence building of employees who acquire a disability through the course of their working lives. We don't need to be 'fixed'. We are not the problem. I bet the funding that Peter Hobbs found to send me on that McAlinden course all those years ago to learn how to present and tell my story has yielded a better return on investment than many an unconscious bias programme.

Henry Ford, the creator of Ford motor cars, supposedly said, 'If I had asked people what they wanted they would have asked for faster horses.' We have lived through an era of asking employers what they want. Most, particularly those without experience of this complex landscape say the same thing: 'faster horses', i.e. better advice on how to monitor their workforces (count us), more line-management training (to learn how to talk to us), advice on how to make adjustments/accommodations (when many of us know what we need). Training non-disabled employees how to work with employees with disability and how to make adjustments/accommodations will only get us so far. My point is about asking the right questions. Not the same ones to the same stakeholders. They tend to yield the same answer and little progress. So for anyone wanting to make change always, always seek out the best questions, not different versions of the same questions.

My final lesson is that life is made easier and more fun by inviting 'positive doers' into your life. People who make things happen, positively. PurpleSpace is surrounded by 'doers' and they can lift you out of challenge. I don't mean it's not OK to be down or so down you don't know the way up again. I have been there, and I will probably go there again before lights out. But the times when I have been certain of what move to make next are largely when I have been in the company of someone who has 'lifted me' in a positive way and shown me that the way forward is often to just 'do' something and to embrace the word 'good' no matter what the challenge in front of me. This lesson has real meaning for so many people from different walks of life. It is not easy. Every day I am tested. Find the positive 'doers'. Their energy will often walk in the room, virtual or otherwise, before they speak.

As you have heard from my story, I will go to the grave remembering the moment when I raged at the world because of the suggestion that I get a little job. In so doing I hope readers also note and feel the love that came from parents and a family ill-equipped for the unexpected life experience that entered their daughter's life. The word fuelled me. Not always in a good way. But for all the challenge I had with the word 'little' the stretch target was in that sentence too: 'job'. Not everyone gets the same 'gift' from their parents.

The job of securing employment rights for people with disabilities around the world is not done yet. It never will be. I just hope I have helped employees with disability in claiming their vital role in this purple leadership space.

Notes

Preface

1 Kate Nash @KateNashOBE. What about we start to light up purple on 3 December? #IDPWD [Twitter] 9 July 2017, twitter.com/KateNashOBE/status/884070282666835969 (archived at https://perma.cc/395H-5NMR)

Mind your language

1 World Bank. Disability Inclusion, 14 April 2022, www.worldbank.org/en/topic/disability#1 (archived at https://perma.cc/ZG3C-U29Y)
2 United Nations. Convention on the Rights of Persons with Disabilities, 6 May, 2022, www.un.org/development/desa/disabilities/convention-on-the-rights-of-persons-with-disabilities.html (archived at https://perma.cc/8HRB-DP79)

Introduction

1 H Rosling, O Rosling and A Rosling Ronnlund (2019) *Factfulness: Ten reasons we're wrong about the world – and why things are better than you think*, Sceptre, London
2 House of Commons. Disability Employment Gap, Seventh Report of Session 2016–17, Work and Pensions Committee, 23 January 2017, publications.parliament.uk/pa/cm201617/cmselect/cmworpen/56/56.pdf (archived at https://perma.cc/5NJ3-GXVG)

Chapter 1

1 Global RA Network. About Arthritis and RA, 2022, globalranetwork. org/project/disease-info/ (archived at https://perma.cc/P6ZX-F3TD)

2 World Health Organization. The Global Burden of Disease Report, Table 7, p 32, 2004, www.who.int/healthinfo/global_burden_disease/ GBD_report_2004update_full.pdf (archived at https://perma.cc/ A25H-ZG7W)

3 UNICEF. Nearly 240 million children with disabilities around the world, press release, 9 November 2021, www.unicef.org/press-releases/ nearly-240-million-children-disabilities-around-world-unicefs-most-comprehensive (archived at https://perma.cc/4BUH-7ERD)

4 Their World. Children with Disabilities, nd, theirworld.org/resources/ children-with-disabilities/ (archived at https://perma.cc/6PBE-TL6V)

5 Their World. Children with Disabilities, nd, theirworld.org/explainers/ children-with-disabilities (archived at https://perma.cc/9NQX-7FVX)

6 Scope. Disability facts and figures, 2021, www.scope.org.uk/media/ disability-facts-figures/ (archived at https://perma.cc/5JE5-S8PY)

7 PurpleSpace. Five Trust Tests, 2021, www.purplespace.org/ home?myhub&selected=5918 (archived at https://perma.cc/J9DU-7Z6F)

8 PurpleSpace. Five Trust Tests, 2021, www.purplespace.org/ home?myhub&selected=5918 (archived at https://perma.cc/BQH2-DPUG)

9 EAP Association. Employee Assistance Programmes, 2013 Market Watch, www.eapa.org.uk/wp-content/uploads/2014/02/UK-EAPA-MARKET-WATCH-REPORT-2013.pdf (archived at https://perma.cc/ V8SD-KD6Q)

10 EAP Association. Financial return on EAPs: How does your organisation compare?, October 2020, www.eapa.org.uk/wp-content/ uploads/2020/10/20-0014-EAPA-UK-ROI-Report-2020-Web.pdf (archived at https://perma.cc/NK6V-LAEY)

Chapter 2

1 S Duckworth. Disabled people are reclaiming the narrative – but there's more to be done, Each Other, 6 January 2021, eachother.org.uk/possibility-with-disability-reclaim-narrative/ (archived at https://perma.cc/2SJB-2JDB)

2 National Institute for Health and Care Excellence (NICE). NHS Statistics, March 2014, www.nice.org.uk/advice/esnm36/chapter/Introduction (archived at https://perma.cc/4DCS-EPQR)

3 RF Modica, KG Lomax, P Batzel and A Cassanas. Impact of systemic juvenile idiopathic arthritis/Still's disease on adolescents as evidenced through social media posts, National Library of Medicine, 13 June 2018, doi: 10.2147/OARRR.S165010, www.ncbi.nlm.nih.gov/pmc/articles/PMC6005297/ (archived at https://perma.cc/9HQL-YJAC)

4 United Nations. Convention on the Rights of Persons with Disabilities, 6 May 2022, www.un.org/development/desa/disabilities/convention-on-the-rights-of-persons-with-disabilities.html (archived at https://perma.cc/8HRB-DP79)

Chapter 3

1 S Fanshawe (2021) *The Power of Difference: Where the complexities of diversity and inclusion meet practical solutions*, Kogan Page, London

2 RD Laing (1967) *Politics of Experience and The Bird of Paradise*, Penguin, London

3 PurpleSpace (2017) Purple Champions and Allies Leaders Guide, www.purplespace.org/download_doc_file.php?doc=da182b1f73eb08e6bf1a82532c6307d4 (archived at https://perma.cc/K22Z-GH4D)

4 PurpleSpace (2017) Purple Champions and Allies Leaders Guide, www.purplespace.org/download_doc_file.php?doc=da182b1f73eb08e6bf1a82532c6307d4 (archived at https://perma.cc/K22Z-GH4D)

5 PurpleSpace (2017) Purple Champions and Allies Leaders Guide, www.purplespace.org/download_doc_file.php?doc=da182b1f73eb08e6bf1a82532c6307d4 (archived at https://perma.cc/K22Z-GH4D)

6   CMS Energy. Careers, CMS website, May 2022, www.cmsenergy.com/careers/default.aspx (archived at https://perma.cc/RE8H-VGQU)

7   CMS Energy's Reverse Mentoring Program Lifts Disability Inclusive Perspectives (2021) https://disabilityin.org/resource/cms-energys-reverse-mentoring-program-lifts-disability-inclusive-perspectives/ (archived at https://perma.cc/J6HD-HE6D)

8   Freshfields Bruckhouse Deringer. Diversity and inclusion: disability, 2022, www.freshfields.com/en-gb/about-us/responsible-business/diversity-and-inclusion/disability/ (archived at https://perma.cc/F66U-BKKK)

9   J Heumann (2021) *Being Heumann: The unrepentant memoir of a disability rights activist*, WH Allen, London

10 TED Talks. www.youtube.com/user/TEDxTalks/featured (archived at https://perma.cc/4GKS-VUG2)

11 Blinkist. More knowledge in less time, www.blinkist.com (archived at https://perma.cc/BUU2-UAAV)

12 Masterclass. Online education streaming platform, www.masterclass.com (archived at https://perma.cc/7CBA-GMA3)

Chapter 4

1   R Kipling (1910) *If*, poem published in *Rewards and Fairies*, Doubleday Page & Co, New York

2   M Oliver (1990) *The Politics of Disablement (Critical Texts in Social Work and the Welfare State)*, Palgrave, London

3   J Morris (1991) *Pride Against Prejudice, Transforming Attitudes to Disability: A personal politics of disability*, The Women's Press Ltd

4   T Shakespeare (2017) *Disability: The basics*, Routledge, London and New York

5   C Woodall (1980) *Disjointed Life*, William Heinemann Ltd, London

6   SL Morgan (2022) *Driving Forwards: A journey of resilience and empowerment after life-changing injury*, Sphere, London

7   Making The Future of Work Inclusive of People With Disabilities (2019) www.ilo.org/wcmsp5/groups/public/---ed_emp/---ifp_skills/documents/publication/wcms_729457.pdf (archived at https://perma.cc/7M3E-FYHH)

8   HRD Connect. The people with disabilities network at P&G, 28 August 2018, www.hrdconnect.com/2018/08/28/people-with-disabilities-at-pg/ (archived at https://perma.cc/F6QN-5MW7)

Chapter 5

1   Speakers Corner. Samantha Renke in conversation with Nick Gold (podcast) 21 April 2021, YouTube, www.youtube.com/watch?v=vUS8KXlGFnI (archived at https://perma.cc/X4EY-B6JC)
2   N Collamer. Proof that volunteering pays off for job hunters, *Forbes*, [blog] 24 June 2013, www.forbes.com/sites/nextavenue/2013/06/24/proof-that-volunteering-pays-off-for-job-hunters/ (archived at https://perma.cc/Y9XE-5LBU)
3   Corporation for National and Community Service. Volunteering as a Pathway to Employment, June 2013, americorps.gov/sites/default/files/evidenceexchange/FR_RE_VolunteeringPathwaytoEmploymentExecutiveSummary_2013_1.pdf (archived at https://perma.cc/Z99S-ER3C)
4   H Jorgensen. Does it pay to volunteer? The relationship between volunteer work and paid work, Center for Economic and Policy Research, June 2013, cepr.net/documents/publications/volunteer-2013-06.pdf (archived at https://perma.cc/79CG-H8DJ)

Chapter 6

1   J Amaechi, J (2021) *The Promises of Giants*, Nicholas Brealey, London

Chapter 7

1   Office for National Statistics. Disability, well-being and loneliness, UK: 2019, www.ons.gov.uk/peoplepopulationandcommunity/healthandsocialcare/disability/bulletins/disabilitywellbeingandlonelinessuk/2019 (archived at https://perma.cc/4SBH-QVNX)

2   PR Clance and S Imes. The imposter phenomenon in high achieving women: dynamics and therapeutic intervention, *Psychotherapy Theory, Research and Practice*, 1978, 15 (3) www.paulineroseclance.com/pdf/ip_high_achieving_women.pdf (archived at https://perma.cc/G224-GU4Y)

3   S Sandberg (2013) *Lean In: Women, work, and the will to lead*, WH Allen, London

4   Ernst & Young. Application tips, nd, www.ey.com/en_uk/careers/students/application-tips (archived at https://perma.cc/WD2W-ASWH)

5   business disability international, www.businessdisabilityinternational.org (archived at https://perma.cc/5JLH-7QH3)

6   Diedrich. How I cope with imposter syndrome while having learning disabilities, Understood, nd, www.understood.org/en/articles/how-i-cope-with-imposter-syndrome-while-having-learning-disabilities (archived at https://perma.cc/6T6B-4ELG)

Chapter 8

1   United Nations. Disability and Employment: Fact Sheet 1, nd, www.un.org/development/desa/disabilities/resources/factsheet-on-persons-with-disabilities/disability-and-employment.html (archived at https://perma.cc/Q9KQ-KZK6)

2   UK Government. The employment of disabled people 2021, 11 February 2022, www.gov.uk/government/statistics/the-employment-of-disabled-people-2021/the-employment-of-disabled-people-2021 (archived at https://perma.cc/D7F4-YBHF)

3   UK Government. The employment of disabled people 2021, 11 February 2022, www.gov.uk/government/statistics/the-employment-of-disabled-people-2021/the-employment-of-disabled-people-2021 (archived at https://perma.cc/D7F4-YBHF)

4   US Bureau of Labor Statistics. Persons with a disability, 24 February 2022, www.bls.gov/news.release/disabl.nr0.htm (archived at https://perma.cc/BZ39-V7WY)

5   R Sharma. News By Numbers: Only 36% of India's 26 million persons with disabilities are employed, 10 June 2021, www.forbesindia.com/

article/news-by-numbers/news-by-numbers-only-36-of-indias-26-million-persons-with-disabilities-are-employed/68441/1 (archived at https://perma.cc/3W5R-5BC9)

6   People Business. Reasonable adjustments for disability: advice for employers, nd, www.peoplebusiness.co.uk/disability-advice-for-employers/ (archived at https://perma.cc/BUJ3-XR83)

7   Business Disability Forum. Where to start, nd, businessdisabilityforum.org.uk/about-us/where-to-start/ (archived at https://perma.cc/6QPV-GVZW)

8   Scott-Parker. Moving from Ad hoc to Streamlined Efficiency: The Lloyds Banking Group Case Study, Business and Disability, December 2014, www.businessanddisability.org/wp-content/uploads/2020/05/LLOYDS-WORKPLACE-ADJUSTMENTS-CASE-STUDY1.pdf (archived at https://perma.cc/SS4Y-3CXF)

9   K Schneider. I said yes to everything for a year and here's what happened, nd, The Muse, www.themuse.com/advice/i-said-yes-to-everything-for-a-year-and-heres-what-happened (archived at https://perma.cc/M2TP-7A6T)

10   S Fanshawe (2021) *The Power of Difference: Where the complexities of diversity and inclusion meet practical solutions*, Kogan Page, London

Chapter 9

1   Disability Ethical AI. [website] disabilityethicalai.org (archived at https://perma.cc/84C8-2YYW)

Chapter 10

1   A Roddick and R Miller (1992) *Body and Soul: How to succeed in business and change the world*, Vermilion, London

2   *Financial Times* (2021) PageGroup's Steve Ingham: 'Get fit, get out, and get on with life again', www.ft.com/content/8338e1aa-2fb4-4376-a322-1725928e3ba4 (archived at https://perma.cc/KW9W-NF6M)

3   B Brown. The power of vulnerability, TED Talk, YouTube, 3 January
    2011, www.youtube.com/watch?v=iCvmsMzlF7o (archived at
    https://perma.cc/QQ52-E7EB)
4   SL Morgan (2022) *Driving Forwards: A journey of resilience and
    empowerment after life-changing injury*, Sphere, London

Chapter 11

1   G McIntyre. What percentage of small businesses fail? (and other
    need-to-know stats), Fundera, 20 November 2020, www.fundera.com/
    blog/what-percentage-of-small-businesses-fail (archived at
    https://perma.cc/S36Q-6XYN)
2   J Cassidy. The disabled influencers making their mark on social media,
    BBC News, 25 February 2021, www.bbc.co.uk/news/business-56073239
    (archived at https://perma.cc/5QFU-P295)
3   J Amaechi (2021) *The Promises of Giants*, Nicholas Brealey, London

Chapter 12

1   K Nash (2014) *Secrets & Big News: Enabling people to be themselves
    at work*, Kate Nash Associates, London
2   BBC Ouch. Why is the disabled pound purple? 21 January 2014,
    www.bbc.co.uk/news/blogs-ouch-25812302 (archived at
    https://perma.cc/GT5Q-SG9H)
3   K Nash (2014) *Secrets & Big News: Enabling people to be themselves
    at work*, Kate Nash Associates, London
4   K Nash (2014) *Secrets & Big News: Enabling people to be themselves
    at work*, Kate Nash Associates, London
5   K Nash (2014) *Secrets & Big News: Enabling people to be themselves
    at work*, Kate Nash Associates, London

Chapter 13

1   N Doyle. Is it the yuk factor? Disability advocacy is growing up, *Forbes*, 22 March 2022, www.forbes.com/sites/drnancydoyle/2022/03/22/ is-it-the-yuk-factor-disabilty-advocacy-is-growing-up/?sh=12d12a297bf7 (archived at https://perma.cc/H34S-55RB)

2   MP Winslow. Reactions to the imputation of prejudice, *Basic and Applied Social Psychology*, 2004, 26 (4), pp 289–297, doi.org/10.1207/ s15324834basp2604_5 (archived at https://perma.cc/QS84-68PT)

3   MP Winslow, A Aaron and EN Amadife (2010) African Americans' lay theories about the detection of prejudice and non prejudice, *Journal of Black Studies*, 29 November 2010, doi.org/10.1177/ 0021934709357025 (archived at https://perma.cc/M5DP-HR6Q)

4   EA McGibbon and JB Etowa (2009) *Anti-racist Health Care Practice*, Canadian Scholars Press, Toronto

5   http://purplegoatagency.com (archived at https://perma.cc/9W5L-5AXJ)

6   J Browne (2014) *The Glass Closet: Why coming out is good business*, WH Allen, London

Chapter 14

1   N Clarkson. How remote working is helping parents, carers and disabled people, Virgin Group, 13 October 2021, www.virgin.com/ about-virgin/latest/how-remote-working-is-helping-parents-carers-and-disabled-people (archived at https://perma.cc/2PP7-DB38)

2   *Financial Times* (2021) PageGroup's Steve Ingham: 'Get fit, get out, and get on with life again', www.ft.com/content/8338e1aa-2fb4-4376-a322-1725928e3ba4 (archived at https://perma.cc/KW9W-NF6M)

3   SE Morris. LinkedIn joins the bandwagon by compensating ERG leaders for culture impacts, *Forbes*, 17 June 2021, www.forbes.com/sites/ simonemorris/2021/06/17/linkedin-joins-the-bandwagon-by-compensating-erg-leaders-for-culture-impacts/ (archived at https://perma.cc/ZQS4-9NWP)

4   Spotlight on HSBC. YouTube, 1 March 2021, www.youtube.com/ watch?v=unnZvNaRung (archived at https://perma.cc/FR4R-NTYF)

Index